PRAIRIE ROOTS:

CALL OF THE WILD

Paul Gruchow
Robert Sayre
Joni L. Kinsey
Mary Swander
Thomas K. Dean
Steve Semken
Howard Vrankin

Ice Cube Press
North Liberty, Iowa

Prairie Roots: Call of the Wild

First Edition
2 4 6 8 9 7 5 3
second printing 2004

ISBN 1-888160-12-8

The Ice Cube Press
205 N Front Street
North Liberty, Iowa 52317-9302
icecube@inav.net
319.626.2055
www.icecubepress.com

Library of Congress Control Number: 2001095308

Manufactured in the United States of America on acid-free, recycled paper meeting library standards.

Permission:
Permission to reprint, "Not So Plain: Art of the American Prairies" granted by the Great Plains Quarterly, at the Center for Plains Studies, which previously appeared in the summer 1995 issue (vol. 15, no. 3)
George & *Julia* by Mary Swander both previously appeared in her book DRIVING THE BODY BACK

Supported in part with a grant from the Iowa Arts Council, a division of the Department of Cultural Affairs.

Thanks go to the Iowa Arts Council, Aid
Association for Lutherans, the Knutson Family Endowment,
as well as the help of Thomas Dean
for generating the energy needed to expand this year's
Harvest Lecture into two days of events.
Of course, the generosity of the talented writers
and artists who have made contributions to this
publication is fantastic. Thanks as well for her artwork,
and advice with the cover to the one and only Laura
Waldo-Semken and where would I be without the
fun smiles of Fenna Marie, bless all of you!
As I take this book to its second printing I would ask all of
you who read this to take a moment to
pause and honor the memory
of Paul Gruchow.

as we begin reflect :

*"There are some who can live without wild things, and
some who cannot. These essays are the delights
and dilemmas of one who cannot."*
—Aldo Leopold

Contents

The Meaning of Natural History

Paul Gruchow

Henry David Thoreau, who just barely qualified for admission, got his formal training at Harvard College. The system of education at Harvard in 1833 emphasized rote memorization and good behavior. Classroom discussion was out of the question, and even lectures by professors were discouraged. The model student was passive, dutiful, worshipped the ancients, and doubted the advisability of anything contemporary—roughly the reverse of contemporary intellectual fashion. You could be punished academically for skipping chapel, wearing a coat of a color other than black (although Thoreau, too poor to afford a new coat, was tolerated for his old green one), and making inappropriate noises in the dining hall. Of the 63 members of Thoreau's class, 44 eventually found themselves subject to disciplinary action by the faculty. Students, not surprisingly, hated the place. During Thoreau's years at Harvard, the system provoked both a petition campaign, which Thoreau supported—students said the place promoted superficial scholarship—and a riot, from which he was absent, and which was suppressed with rigor a banana republic dictator might have admired. The leaders of the revolt were prosecuted in public court, and the entire sophomore class, with three exceptions, were expelled. The curriculum, designed mainly to turn out ministers, emphasized the study of classical languages, mathematics, and philosophy. Modern languages, although not yet academically respectable in the 1830s, were offered as electives. In addition to the mandatory Greek and Latin, in which he became fluent, Thoreau studied Italian, French, German, and Spanish. The English instruction was not in literature—post-Roman writing was not respectable then either—but in rhetoric. Thoreau had only one class in modern literature—on German and Scandinavian writing, taught by Henry Wadsworth Longfellow—and a single class in biology, a natural history term taught by the college librarian, for whom the subject was an avocation. Both were ventures beyond the required curriculum. Thoreau was, by the standards of his time, a competent student, graduating in the upper third of his class. His teachers thought him an able, if not outstanding, scholar. He might have become a good entomologist if Emerson hadn't spoiled him, his natural history teacher said. His Greek professor, Cornelius Conway Felton, later president of Harvard, remembered him as a scholar of talent, but of such pertinacious oddity in literary matters, that his writing will probably never do him any justice The most promising writer in Thoreau's class, his English professor judged, was one Horace Morison, whose sole work, Pebbles From the Seashore, you surely must know. Harvard did offer, despite its deficiencies as an educational institution, a splendid library of 50,000 volumes, which Thoreau patronized for the rest of his days. There he began his lifelong habit of far-flung and systematic reading. During his college years he read his way through the 21-volume Chalmers anthology, The English Poets. He studied the Greek poets, read Shakespeare and Homer, devoured travel books, and sampled the works of such contemporary American writers as Cooper, Irving, and Longfellow. Later, his reading would expand to include works of science and natural history, of religion and philosophy, and such accounts of native American life and culture as were then available. He read not only in English, but also in the six languages he had learned at college, and, more haltingly, in Sanskrit and Hebrew. Thoreau not only read voraciously, but he began in college to keep the extensive notebooks—a million words of which still survive—on which he drew when he settled into his life's work. He also began, in college, the practice of slipping away into the nearby woods and fields to see what was up in nature. One winter while he was at Harvard, he made daily visits to the nest of a weasel in the hollow of an old apple tree. When his neighbor and mentor, Ralph Waldo Emerson, suggested to the young graduate that he make his journal systematic—the date was October 22, 1837—the tools of Thoreau's intellectual life were complete. From then on, with remarkable steadfastness of purpose, he practiced a threefold discipline: mornings for writing, afternoons for walking, evening for reading and reflection. Over the next twenty-some years, he wrote an immortal book; started, with his brother, an elementary school that was a hundred years ahead of its time; designed the best pencil then available; made still-reliable surveys of the countryside around Concord, Massachusetts; kept a three-million-word journal that is in itself one of the monuments of American culture; and, we have only recently learned, left behind at his premature death the first serious work of ecology, although the scientific idea of ecology had not yet been invented.

John Muir, born in Scotland, was raised at hard labor on the Wisconsin frontier by a father who was tyrannical, anti-intellectual, and a religious extremist. Forbidden to read in the evenings, Muir found an outlet for his lively intelligence in invention. He experimented with waterwheels and windmills and then with a series of remarkable clocks, all of the pieces whittled from hickory, which he assembled with the aid only of a book that taught him the laws of the pendulum. He was forbidden to take apart the family clock to see firsthand how these devices were conventionally made. The first of his clocks was shaped like a sawmill and not only kept time but registered dates, lit fires and a lamp, and could be set to upend a bed at any hour. Muir called it his early rising machine. He made a clock shaped like a scythe, in which each individual part also had the shape of a scythe or of an arrow: it kept accurate time for more than fifty years. And he made a clock meant to be hung from the barn and designed to be read from the adjacent fields: its main hand was fourteen feet long; but his father, fearing that it would attract crowds, refused to let him install it. Muir also made thermometers, pyrometers, hygrometers and a barometer as a youth. Among these was a thermometer built on the same scale as the barn clock, mounted high on the Muir house, and so sensitive that it registered the body heat of a person approaching to within four or five feet of it. An equally sensitive thermometer, fashioned from an old washboard, and two of his early rising machines became Muir's ticket to freedom. He demonstrated these devices at the Temple of Art at the Wisconsin State Fair in 1860. They caused a public sensation, won a prize, and landed him a job with another inventor who was exhibiting a steam-powered ice boat at the fair. Muir was to tend the boat in exchange for lessons in mechanical drawing, which he never got. Trial runs that winter at Prairie du Chien, Wisconsin, on the Mississippi, proved the boat a flop, and Muir soon departed for the University of Wisconsin in Madison, "desperately hungry and thirsty for knowledge," he said, "and willing to endure anything to get it." He was admitted there, despite his paucity of formal education, as a first year student, enrolled in chemistry, geology, Latin, and Greek, the science courses for himself, the language courses for his mother, who hoped he would become a preacher. He was conspicuous on campus for his homespun dress and his unshorn and unkempt hair and beard, but he was also soon marked as the best chemistry student at the university and became locally celebrated for his inventions. These included a new early rising machine, a bed triggered by sunlight to dump its occupant onto the floor; a loafer's chair rigged so that sitting in it fired off a pistol loaded with a blank cartridge; and a study desk run by a clock that dropped a book onto a shelf, gave the user a predetermined number of minutes to examine it, and then swept it aside to be replaced with another. Students showing parents and dignitaries the campus sights invariably took them around to see Muir and his inventions. But he had no money, and the Civil War, which Muir spent in Canada, intervened. In the end, he completed only two-and-a-half years of work at the University. After he left Madison, Muir wandered and botanized along the Canadian shores of the Great Lakes, and did factory work, inventing, on speculation in the finished products, machines that doubled the standard rate of production of hardwood broom handles and rake teeth. Before the 30,000 broom handles and 6,000 rakes he had made could be sold, the factory burned, destroying not only his inventory but also his notebooks and herbaria. In 1866, with just enough money for his train fare, he returned to the United States, getting as far as Indianapolis, where he found work in a factory making carriage parts. His extraordinary abilities as a technical manager were soon noticed, and Muir was given wide latitude to make improvements. He invented machinery to make complete wheels, except for the iron tires, without hand labor. He improved the efficiency of the system of belts that operated the equipment, did time and motion studies—these were among the first such studies ever done—leading to improvements in the organization of the plant, and recommended shorter work days for laborers. Ten-hour days were then standard, and were still regarded as an extremely liberal concession to labor, but Muir showed that the precipitous drop in efficiency after the first eight hours made longer days counterproductive. But Muir disregarded his own advice. One day in March of 1867, while working alone late at night on a new belt in the factory, he lost his grip on the file he was using and it flew up and pierced his right eye, which went blind. He recuperated for a month. Eventually the sight returned to his eye, but his factory days, which had brought him up against what he called "the gobble gobble school of economics," were over. When he had sufficiently recovered from his accident, he set out on foot, walked a thousand miles to Miami, caught a boat to Cuba, where his plan to continue on the South America was foiled by a bout with malaria, went to California instead, by way of Panama, got off his ship in San Francisco, walked straight through the town and into the Sierra Nevada mountains, and never looked back. Muir wandered the Sierras alone for months at a stretch, eager to experience everything they had to offer, to the extent of riding out a thunderstorm in the top of a tall spruce tree, just to see what that would be like. He learned, he said, that even trees do a good bit of traveling. He figured out the role of glaciation in shaping the Sierras, his work proving more accurate than that of the leading American scientist of the day, Louis Aggasiz, who was also wrong, unlike Muir, about Darwin. He wrote several enduring volumes of natural history, campaigned for the formation of the national park system, founded the Sierra Club, and prospered as one of the first big fruit growers in California's Central Valley.

Rachel Carson grew up in the countryside near Pittsburgh, Pennsylvania. She was a sickly child who frequently missed school and perhaps on that account was something of a loner. She found companionship in the woods and fields surrounding her home. She was also precocious, sailing through her schooling, which included a degree in biology, magna cum laude, from the Pennsylvania College for Women; a postgraduate internship at the Marine Biological Laboratory at Woods Hole, where she saw the ocean for the first time; and a Master's Degree in zoology, with a concentration in genetics, from Johns Hopkins University. Carson, knowing from an early age that she wanted to be a writer, enrolled, when she entered the Philadelphia College for Women, as an English major. In her junior year she took the introductory biology courses to fulfill a distribution requirement, expecting to find the experience distasteful. But she loved the classes so much that, to the dismay of her English Department mentor, for whom she was the star student, she switched her major at the last minute, and over the next several years gave little further thought to writing. One would not have been encouraged to believe in an English Department in the 1920s that science could be a suitable subject for literature. Indeed, although a strong case can be made that the two distinctive contributions of American writers to literature are the short story and the natural history essay, it is still true that Literature, when it is thought of with a capital L, means poems, novels, and plays. The essay is still treated as the literary equivalent of an etude in music, a minor form, suitable for use in instructing the young, but not in itself of any serious artistic or intellectual interest. Carson emerged from college in the first years of the Great Depression when employment of any kind was hard to find, much less for a woman scientist. She had the good luck, however, to interview with Elmer Higgens of the U.S. Bureau of Fisheries, a distinguished biologist but no writer, who had just been assigned the task of writing a series of radio scripts about the Bureau's work. When he learned that Carson could write, Higgens took a gamble and hired her. The radio series proved so successful that Higgens edited the scripts into a government booklet, asking Carson for an introduction. He rejected the text she produced, telling her it was too good for a government pamphlet, and urging her to send it instead to the *Atlantic Monthly*. Carson, who knew that the magazine had also published Thoreau and Muir, did not have as much confidence in her work as her employer. She filed the piece away in a desk drawer. In the meantime, her father and older sister died, and Carson took on the task of supporting her family, augmenting her income at the Bureau with part-time teaching at the University of Maryland. When a position opened as a junior aquatic biologist in the Bureau, she took the Civil Service test, earned the highest score, and was hired and assigned as assistant editor in the Information Section. Her radio scripts had by then attracted the attention of the Sunday editor of the *Baltimore Sun*, who signed her on as an occasional contributor. Her success there finally gave her the courage to send the introduction she had tucked away to the Atlantic Monthly. The magazine bought it, the piece led to a contract with Simon and Schuster, and that resulted, in November, 1941, in the publication of Under the Sea Wind, regarded by some critics as her best book. It got lost, however, in the national trauma of the opening days of World War II, attracted little notice, and sold poorly. The Bureau Of Fisheries became the U.S. Fish and Wildlife Service. Carson rose steadily through its ranks, becoming, by 1947, editor in chief of the Information Division. Her wartime duties included writing a series of pamphlets on the cooking of various seafoods, which the government was promoting as an alternative to the increasingly scarce supply of red meats. This assignment amused her co-workers, who knew that she abhorred all housework, and especially loathed cooking. During the 1940s, as Carson worked by day at the Fish and Wildlife Service, Carson also moonlighted as a free-lancer for several national magazines, nurturing the ambition to write another book. The idea she settled on, and got a contract for from Oxford University Press, was to write a biography of the sea. She had looked for such a book, she said, and had not been able to find it, as, of course, she couldn't: the idea was as radically original as Thoreau's Walden. With The Sea Around Us, as the book came eventually to be called, Carson was inventing an entirely new kind of nature writing. She labored at the book through the late 1940s, writing at home far into the night after she had come home from her day job. She was a slow and meticulous writer, a perfectionist not only about her style but also about her facts. The book synthesized information gathered from hundreds of dense texts and obscure scientific articles, and from correspondence with marine biologists and oceanographers around the world. It was to be an unusual book not only in its biographical form but also in that it was primarily based not on firsthand observation but on library work, although she did supplement it with as much field investigation as she could find the time for, learning, among other things in the course of her preparations, to scuba dive. Carson was to the literature of natural history what her contemporary I.F. Stone was to political journalism, a writer whose authority derived not from being an eyewitness—a notably unreliable kind of testimony, in any case—but on having read all the fine print that everybody else skipped. Even before The Sea Around Us was published in 1951, it attracted significant attention, earning her a fellowship for promising young writers and a $1,000 prize, for an excerpt published in the Yale Review, as the best science writing of 1950. But Carson's big break came in the spring of 1951, when the New Yorker published three long and celebrated excerpts from the book under the title Profiles From the Sea. When the book was finally launched in July of 1951, it landed straight on the best-seller lists, and stayed there for the next 83 weeks. What is more, Oxford University Press reissued Under the Sea Wind the next year and it, too, became a best-seller, making Carson one of those rare writers to have two simultaneous best-sellers, a feat normally reserved to the John Grishams and Danielle Steeles of the world. From then on, she was showered with invitations to speak and publish, with prizes and honorary degrees. Carson at first shied away from doing the book that altered contemporary history. With her literary success, she had been able to quit her job and to buy a house in Maine on the shore of the ocean she loved so much. After a third book on the subject, The Edge of the Sea, which started as a conventional guidebook and evolved into an account of three shoreline ecosystems, one of the first books of this kind, Carson felt she had done what she could with the sea as a subject. She considered writing a book about evolution and decided against it. While she was still mulling the possibilities for a new subject, one of her friends sent her a copy of a letter she had sent to the Boston Globe, protesting the aerial spraying of Cape Cod with DDT to control mosquitoes. Carson looked into the practice, was disturbed by what she learned, and wrote a magazine piece on the dangers of—overusing DDT, but editors found it unconvincing—it was scientifically unorthodox—and nobody was willing to take the piece. Then, in 1957, the government announced plans to spray Long Island with DDT to control gypsy moths. Carson, who knew that gypsy moths are forest creatures and that Long Island is not forested, found this idea absurd. A group of Long Islanders sued to prevent the spraying. Carson wrote to E. B. White, suggesting that he cover the trial. White replied that she ought to do it herself, so she made plans to write about the trial for the New Yorker and to collect the pieces in a small volume. She set out, as she had done with the sea, to master her subject, reading everything she could find, ferreting through journals in medicine, organic chemistry, agronomy, and other disciplines, and initiating correspondence with scientists all over the world who might shed some light on the matter. Before long, what had been meant to be a brief collection of essays blossomed into a full-scale examination of the ecological implications of pesticides. Carson was not the first person to address this issue. There had been other books, but they had been either eloquent books written by authors with a shaky grasp of science, or books of sound scientific analysis written by authors with no literary ability. Carson brought a unique combination of assets to the work: she had enough training to read and understand the science, she was scrupulous about the details, she was by nature a synthesizer rather than a reductionist, she was a gifted writer, and she commanded, on the strength of three best-selling books, a huge audience. She was also aware, by the time she was finishing Silent Spring, that she was dying of cancer and that the book would certainly be her last testament; the underlying tone of urgency in the book is one factor in its great power. When it appeared in 1962, Silent Spring had a bigger impact than Carson could ever have imagined. Although it was vigorously, even viciously, and nearly unanimously attacked in scientific circles as the work of an hysterical amateur, with such effectiveness that even today it will occasionally be asserted by an environmentalist with the stature of a Bill McKibben that Carson was not a scientist, the book, precisely because it was scientifically sound, held and took root. It changed attitudes not only about pesticides, but about the earth itself, and about science, and was the critical spark that ignited the environmental movement that has endured now for three generations.

Edward O. Wilson had the quintessential naturalist's childhood. He grew up, that is, poor, lonely, socially an outsider. His father was an itinerant government accountant, constantly on the move. Wilson's elementary and secondary education took place in fifteen or sixteen schools. During that last eight of those years, the family moved from one city to another ten times, often lodging in boarding houses. In the summers he was farmed out to family friends in Alabama, Florida, Virginia, Maryland, and the District of Columbia. He was perpetually the new kid on the block. He was, moreover, somewhat deaf; he had blinded one eye as a young boy when he collided with the sharp spine of a panfish; and he was slightly built: hardly the sort of boy to make his way in the sports-minded culture of his peers. There was no educational theory in 1938, he remarks in his autobiography, "to suggest that loneliness in a beautiful environment might be a good if risky way to create a scientist, at least a field biologist." There is no such educational theory now, either, but that formula might describe the childhood of most important naturalists in American literature. There is, I might note parenthetically, one other striking convergence in the biographies of naturalists. In nearly every instance, lurking somewhere in the background, there is an absent, or tortured, or ineffectual father. Thoreau's father was affable and inept. Muir's father prayed in his study while his boys cleared the land and ran the family farm. About Carson's father, her biographers mention only his name; there would seem to have been little else to tell. Wilson's father was alcoholic, suffered from ulcers and acute chronic bronchitis brought on by a three-pack-a-day cigarette habit, and ultimately committed suicide. I do not know what to make of this except to observe that the human consolation found in nature is among the most compelling self-interested arguments against destroying it. Wilson knew by the time he was a teenager that he wanted to spend his life as a field biologist. His monaural vision and impaired hearing ruled out birds, amphibians, and most mammals, but the sight in his good eye, it turned out, was not only undamaged but hyperacute. He was equipped to study small things. So insects it would be, he decided. Not butterflies. Too much was already known about them, and there were many excellent lepidopterists at work. Flies, he thought, would be the ideal choice: he found them beautiful, they existed everywhere in great diversity, and most of them had not yet been identified, much less studied. He sent off for the necessary supplies. But the Second World War was just beginning, Czechoslovakia's borders were already closed to international trade, and the long black mounting pins he needed were made there. He would have to settle for a subject he could collect and preserve with supplies available at the local drug store. And so it was that he became a specialist in ants. Eventually Wilson learned more about ants than any other human being, and his curiosity about them led him far beyond his nominal subject. His interest in their evolution led him to name and essentially to found the field of evolutionary biology. His interest in their patterns of distribution ultimately inspired the theory of island biogeography, one of the seminal theoretical ideas of twentieth century biology. His interest in the social organization of ants led him to coin the word "biophilia" and to advance a theory of sociobiology, an idea that has been bitterly opposed, but mainly on ideological rather than on evidentiary grounds. His work on ants led him to the tropical rainforests of the world, with which he fell in love, and his grief over their widespread destruction prompted him, late in life, to become a social activist and, in this role, a popularizer of the idea of biodiversity, a word that did not exist fifteen years ago and which is now part of the vocabulary of every educated citizen on the planet. Despite his lifelong sinecure in an elite institution—Harvard University—and despite his path-breaking work on several frontiers of biological science, Wilson, when he recently published his autobiography , gave it the unassuming, indeed old-fashioned, title Naturalist. In it, he writes that he never thought of his work in any other terms, that he always wanted to be simply a discoverer, dazzled by the variety of nature, and thrilled by any new discovery of even such a modest sort as the discovery of a new species of ant.

These four writers—Henry David Thoreau, John Muir, Rachel Carson, and Edward O. Wilson—span a century and a half during which science, in the contemporary sense, emerged from its infancy and developed into the primary intellectual force of our time. In terms of our assumptions about the nature of the world, Thoreau entered his adult life closer to the Paleolithic than to the twenty-first century. The rapturous writings in his journals about the railroad and the telegraph wire—he was not simple-mindedly anti-technological—reflect the fact that each was, in his lifetime, a revolutionary invention. Thoreau lived barely long enough to have heard of Darwin, and even Wilson remembers, in his autobiography, a time an astonishingly few years ago when a proposal to hire one ecologist at Harvard University was regarded as an outrageous venture into hokum. Everybody at Harvard who counted knew, as recently as the late 1970s, that the future of science lay in molecular biology and not in the study of biological systems or in the work of taxonomists like Wilson, whom his condescending colleague James Watson referred to as stamp collectors. Although these writers represent very different stages of our recent past; were as divergent in temperament as any four human beings one might choose at random; traveled, literally and figuratively, in quite different realms; and ranged in formal training from Wilson's Ivy League Ph.D. to Muir's essentially grammar school education, they shared several key intellectual qualities that illuminate not only their work but the larger role of literary natural historians in our culture. These writers were all, for one thing, generalists rather than narrow specialists. Thoreau's famous remark, "I have traveled much, in Concord," might well stand as their intellectual credo. It was not that they didn't delve deeply into their chosen subjects. Thoreau kept elaborate phenologies of the blooming of the plants in the vicinity of Concord and spent ten years assiduously tracing the dispersal of every kind of seed he could find within a day's walk of his house. Muir planted stakes in the glaciers of the Sierra Nevadas and traced their movements inch by inch through many years in his effort to understand how they worked and what influence they had on the surrounding landscape. Carson may have set some kind of record for the reading of arcane journal articles in dozens of highly technical specialties. Wilson, as a young scientist, literally circled the globe in search of every kind of ant he could find. These were not merely stamp collectors. Nor is it the case that these thinkers rejected the reductionist premise of science, the notion that you can learn something valid about a whole system by examining closely its parts, the idea so central to the intellectual movement know as the Enlightenment and to the industrial revolution that it spawned. One argument now commonly advanced is that holism—the notion that the system rather than the individual is the basic unit of reality and that this reality embodies something larger than the sum of its parts—is a viable, indeed necessary, replacement for reductionism. The problem is, of course, that the choice—reductionism or holism—is a false choice.

It is entirely probable that both points of view offer versions of the truth that are, at once, useful and, taken exclusively, misleading; that a vision of life embracing its real complexity will be neither reductionist nor holistic, but something else altogether, arrived at in the synthesis of these points of view, together with as many others as we can imagine. The task of making sense of the world does not so much lie in finding the a supposedly single "correct" perspective as in learning to assimilate many perspectives, reductionism and holism among them. The obvious problem with reductionism is that it fails to account for the effects of synergy, or, as a geneticist might say, of pleiotropy. The obvious problem with holism, on the other hand, is that it fails to account for the ways in which the system itself may be radically altered by the random influence of any one of its parts. If holism alone were true, we ought to be able, by now, to predict accurately next Monday's weather. If reductionism alone were true, we ought to be able to solve the nation's crime problem by building more prisons. The genius of the four writers I am discussing is that they worked reductively—which is the only practical possibility, since no human being yet born has been able to think about the whole world all at once—but did not stop there. They were all, by temperament, despite their methods of working, synthesizers. You can tell a lot about how a clock works by taking it apart and examining its pieces, but if you never put it back together again, your knowledge will not result in a more accurate sense of time. These writers were specialists who thought to try to reassemble the pieces of their work. They had a talent for generalization and the courage to indulge in it.

They were all intellectuals, moreover, with a democratic temperament. They assumed their ideas could and ought to be communicated to a general audience. Even Wilson, when he sat down to write an encyclopedic survey of all that is known about ants, a subject one would hardly think suitable for wide dissemination, took such care with his work and wrote so accessibly that the resulting volume won a Pulitzer Prize in literature. These were not writers to hide in thickets of jargon, or to be content with publishing their ideas in places where only their colleagues would be likely to see them. They did not mistake obscurity of expression for depth of vision. In a time when scientific information is increasingly offered as an exclusive substitute not only for other kinds of learning but also for any conversation that is not strictly technical, these writers made a principled effort to include citizens at large in the discussion and provoked widespread debate about issues of science and technology. A long line of critics, especially of literary critics who have been bored with his interest in nature, have painted Thoreau as a cranky misogynist who advocated that everybody retire to a hermitage, but the central question he raised remains urgently relevant: What, he asked, is the relationship between technological (or material) advancement and human happiness, and what would be required for the former to enhance the latter? Muir was the first, and in some ways is still the loudest, critic of the U.S. Forest Service's multiple use policy. Are there, he asked, any long-term values in nature that transcend their short-term exploitation? Carson raised the central power question: Can nature be overwhelmed, she asked, or must it be accommodated? What sort of victory, she asked, can we expect from a war with nature? What, Wilson asks, is the relationship between nature and culture? Both have co-evolved through at least the last ten thousand years. Would it be helpful to know how each has influenced the other? These are serious questions with profound consequences for the planet's future, and not one of them can be answered by resort to technicalities alone. Not one of these questions would yield a publishable article in a refereed scientific journal, although much that is published in such journals could shed some light on the possibilities. They are questions that overreach the limits of the demonstrable. One challenge that these writers pose is whether we can afford a system of scholarship that, at its highest levels, actively discourages asking the biggest questions. Particularly with respect to technology, we now frequently face that conundrum in which technologists disavow responsibility for the social consequences of their inquiries and inventions, claiming, quite properly, that such matters ought to be discussed by society as a whole, while at the same time communicating their own knowledge in language unintelligible, in many cases, even to other scientists outside their specialties and, at the same time, branding anybody who sees any negative implication in their work as unscientific, or

Luddite, or a threat to the freedom of scientific inquiry. Rachel Carson's challenge to the indiscriminate use of certain kinds of pesticides was not generally answered in the scientific community with countervailing scientific evidence but by just such ad hominen attacks. Were it not for the intervention of scientifically literate thinkers like Carson, whose fates are independent of their curricula vitae, we might be obliged to accept all scientific and technological developments on faith, just as the medieval faithful, deprived of the Bible in the vernacular, were obliged to accept all theology as divinely inspired. The natural historians, in our culture, have been the democratizers of science and technology.

They have been, as well, the keepers of the pre-Enlightenment idea that, in the largest sense, there is only one earth history, and that is natural history. For a time we were inclined to forget that, although we are creatures of culture, and culture is an artifact of the mind, the mind itself is a biological organ, and that we cannot, therefore, escape our common heritage with the rest of life. Death is nature's way of reminding us that we are, after all, creatures and not gods. There is a wonderful Blackfeet myth that expresses this truth. In the beginning, in the Blackfeet story of the creation, as in so many accounts of the origins of life on earth, including the modern scientific one, there was water. One day Old Man decided to find out what lay beneath the water. So he sent down diving animals on reconnaissance: a duck, an otter, a beaver, a badger; they all dived in vain. Then he sent down a muskrat, which returned with a lump of mud in its paws. When the Old Man blew upon it, the mud swelled up until it became the earth. Old Man traveled the length and breadth of the new earth, piling up stones to make mountains, digging rivers and lakes and filling them with water, creating grasses to cover the prairies, and trees to shade the forests, and birds and animals of every kind. Then he made for himself a wife, Old Woman, who was very clever. The two of them decided together how people should be made. Old Man insisted on having first say in everything, which Old Woman agreed to, so long as she could have last say. People should have eyes and mouths, arranged vertically on their faces, Old Man said. Fine, said his wife, but they should be situated crosswise. They should have ten fingers on each hand. Fingers they shall have, Old Woman said, but so many would be awkward; let people have four fingers and a thumb on each hand. Then came the big question: Should they live forever or should people die? "I'll toss a buffalo chip on the water," Old Man said. "If it floats, people shall die four days and then rise again. If it sinks, people shall die."

"As you wish," Old Woman said, "but let me toss a stone into the water instead." The stone, of course, sank, and so it was decided that people should die. Old Man and Old Woman agreed that this was for the best. If they should never die, they said, then people would never feel sorry for one another.

The great contemporary oceanographer Sylvia Earle suggests another context in which our own history might be understood. If the history of the earth were to be represented, she says, on a scale equal to the depth of the deepest ocean, human civilization would occur only in the last inch, equal to the depression a floating gull makes on the surface of the sea. By insisting, through a long moment of hubris, on the reality that human history is a branch of natural history, the literary natural historians have been nurturers and preservers of the very possibility of history.

These writers also share in a refusal to acknowledge the distinction, alive since the Age of Enlightenment, between the sciences and the humanities. The extremes are best represented by Thoreau, whose apprenticeship was as a poet, and Wilson, whose earliest interests were exclusively scientific. Thoreau worried in his journal that his poetry would be overwhelmed by his science. He thought science, in itself, a barren enterprise, but he thought poetry written on instinct alone equally so. "At first blush," he said, "a man is not capable of reporting truth; he must be drenched and saturated with it first. What was enthusiasm in the young man must become temperament in the mature man. Without excitement, heat, or passion, he will survey the world which excited the youth and threw him off his balance… . A style in which matter is all in all, and the manner nothing at all." Thoreau insisted, like a good scientist, that a writer's work ought to be founded upon facts, but, more than that, upon such facts as the writer has had occasion personally to verify. He also insisted, like a good humanitarian, indeed like a good deconstructionist humanitarian, that those facts were useless until they had been established in some context that revealed their significance. "Facts," he wrote in his journal, "should be only as the frame to my pictures; ... facts to tell who I am, and where I have been or what I have thought; as now the bell rings for the evening meeting, and its volumes of sound, like smoke which rises where a cannon is fired, make the tent in which I dwell. My facts shall be falsehood to the common sense. I should so state the facts that they shall be significant, shall be myths or mythologic." We now assume, tragically—for myths are among the highest expressions of the human imagination—that myths are by definition false, but what Thoreau was talking about, in essence, was the social construction of reality, which he believed to be of a higher order of truth than the mere facts. Here Thoreau predicts, as he foreshadowed so many ideas in our culture, Foucault. Wilson writes in his autobiography about being powerfully impressed as an undergraduate student by Erwin Schrodinger's What is Life?, which argued that it is nothing more than a physical process, entirely explicable by the laws of physic and chemistry; and by Ernst Mayr's Systematics and the Origin of Species, which offered a keystone synthesis of genetics and evolutionary theory. For Wilson, "Science became the new light and the way." Still, he remembered that he had experienced a Christian conversion only three years earlier. "Religion, I knew from personal experience," he writes, "is a perpetual fountainhead of human emotion. It cannot be dismissed as superstition. It cannot be compartmentalized as the manifestation of some separate world. From the beginning I could never accept that science and religion are separate domains, with fundamentally different questions and answers. This Wilson says, looking back on a lifetime of science, is still the view he holds. And it has been, in general, the view of the literary natural historians, who have always walked with one foot in science and the other in the humanities, unwilling to relinquish either, valuing both for their revealing disparities of method, but refusing to see them as concerned with fundamentally different questions and answers. Current trends in literary theory, in particular, apply self-consciously scientific models to the methods of the humanities, threatening to make even the arts into subjects so arcane, rarified, and specialized as to preclude the legitimate interest of ordinary human beings. It may well happen, if this movement continues to flourish, that, just as the writers I have been discussing have kept history alive, so their successors will preserve what used to be thought of as the humanities, rather as monks copied out the classical texts in anticipation of the Renaissance, against that dark time when we will have specialized ourselves into utter incoherence.

I would, finally, mark this about the literary natural historians: they are all, to the last one, celebrants of wonder. There is not a cynic in the lot. "A child's world," Rachel Carson wrote, "is fresh and new and beautiful, full of wonder and excitement. It is our misfortune that for most of us that clear-eyed vision, that true instinct for what is beautiful and awe-inspiring, is dimmed and even lost before we reach adulthood. If I had influence with the good fairy who is supposed to preside over the christening of all children, I should ask that her gift to each child in the world be a sense of wonder so indestructible that it would last throughout life, as an unfailing antidote against the boredom and disenchantment of later years, the sterile preoccupation with things that are artificial, the alienation from our sources of strength." Good science in our time is anti-mystical, and good humanities scholarship is anti-romantic. We fear above all else, as scholars, that we might be caught in an unguarded moment of sentiment or nostalgia. The great sin of our age is to think fondly of the past. But in the world of the gene, in our biology, we are inextricably bound to the very beginnings of life. To despise the past, therefore—to suppose that our highest intellectual goal is to debunk all that has gone before us—is to despise ourselves. There is no higher or miserable arrogance than that which denies our beginnings. To wonder, to be astonished, to feel awe, is the beginning of a suitable humility. "Whatever attitude to human existence you fashion for yourself, know that it is valid only if it be the shadow of an attitude to Nature," Henry Beston wrote. His words might serve to summarize this whole intellectual tradition. "A human life," he wrote, "so often likened to a spectacle upon a stage, is more justly a ritual. The ancient values of dignity, beauty, and poetry which sustain it are of Nature's inspiration; they are born of the mystery and beauty of the world. Do no dishonour to the earth lest you dishonour the spirit of man. Hold your hands out over the earth as over a flame. To all who love her, who open to her the doors of their veins, she gives of her strength, sustaining them with her own tremor of dark life. Touch the earth, love the earth, honour the earth, her plains, her valleys, her hills, and her seas; rest your spirit in her solitary places. For the gifts of life are the earth's and they are given to all, and they are the songs of birds at daybreak, Orion and the Bear, and dawn seen over ocean from the beach."

Squaring Off

Robert Sayre

The most obvious feature of the Middle Western landscape, as opposed to the giant prairie landscape that it replaced, is also a symbol of its monotony and uniformity. I mean "the Grid," or the way all the land is boxed into one-mile squares that make it appear from an airplane flying over it at 35,000 feet like graph paper or a giant, endless checkerboard. Nothing could be more unnatural, and it sometimes seems to objectify all that everyone insultingly asserts about the land's and the culture's dullness and predictability. Columbus, Ohio to Denver, Colorado, land and people alike are Squares.

I did not become aware of "the Grid," however, until about a year after I got my driver's licence. Then, during a Christmas vacation in 1950 a friend and I were driving around, he in his family's 1950 Chevrolet with an automatic shift and I in my family's 1949 Ford with manual shift. We started drag racing, but quickly realized it was dangerous and might get us arrested. So we drove out into the flat country north and east of Columbus where we found straight, deserted roads, and there we soon discovered, as we sped from intersection to intersection, that all the roads were exactly a mile apart. We did not have to race against each other; we could race against the clock, on these "measured miles," as we called them, that the Ohio Highway Department had obligingly laid out for us.

Somewhat later, we learned what every Midwesterner should know: that these roads were a mile apart and ran at right angles to one another, north-south and east-west, because they were laid out on the old surveyors' section lines that divided all the land into mile-square "sections" of 640 acres each. This was why the roads in that part of Franklin County did not go on diagonals or twist and turn (as we sometimes wished they did, when we wanted to have road races), and it was also why the roads seemed to have no destinations. They did not go from town to town but simply on and on, crossing one road after another, until they finally ended at a T intersection or a major highway.

Like all drivers in the Middle West, we also eventually became frustrated because the absence of diagonal roads often made travel longer. One had to move at right angles, like a rook on a chess board; one could seldom go on the hypotenuse.

Yet as I have learned to live in Iowa and put up with the Grid, I have also tried to learn more of its history and to realize the hundreds of other ways in which it affects our lives. Because it organizes the direction of roads in town as well as in the country, and therefore the location of houses on rectangular north-south or east-west lots, it affects us every day, from the moment we wake up. Our east windows face due east, our west ones due west. So we in the Midwest are also likely to be much more aware of the cardinal directions, to think of them as we move about, and use them in giving directions to another person. The Grid also profoundly affects our agriculture, ecology, and economy, as I have come to realize. And yet, because it is such a basic part of our lives, we think it is "natural" and fail to keep in mind what a highly artificial construction it is, the triumph, as some one said, of geometry over topography. At the same time, whether we take it for granted and like it, or notice it and complain about it, we fail to appreciate what an awesome, man-made wonder it is.

Gertrude Stein, who saw the Middle West from an early commercial airplane when she was lecturing in the United States in 1935, grasped its artificial— and artistic—quality when she said it made the land look like a Cubist painting. Stein had a foreign and modernist perspective, as did the English-born geographer, Norman Thrower, who could not understand why the pilot on a plane from Los Angeles to Kansas patriotically pointed out the Grand Canyon but then had said not one word about the mathematically demarcated landscape of Kansas. Why was the Grand Canyon, a work of nature, a national symbol, while the much greater landscape of Kansas, a work of man and the national government, was not?[1]

The rectangular or cadastral survey, as geographers call it, actually takes in much more than just Kansas and the Middle West. It covers 70% of the lower forty-eight states, in fact. But we associate it with the Middle West because it is most visible here, so that nowhere else in the world can one see so much land so organized. It is as unique as that other famous

American grid, Manhattan Island, but whereas Manhattan was divided up mainly for economic convenience (like the page of an account book, Henry James said) the survey of the Western Territory had a political and philosophical basis as well. Indeed, it was a cosmic union of Jeffersonian agrarianism and economic expediency, put together with mathematical precision.

Jefferson's most famous statement of his agrarian philosophy is in Notes on the State of Virginia, where he advocates that Americans not try to rival Europe in manufacturing. "...We have an immensity of land courting the industry of the husbandman," he wrote, and he wanted "our citizens" to improve it.

Those who labour in the earth are the chosen people of God, if ever he had a chosen people, whose breasts he has made his peculiar deposit for substantial and genuine virtue. It is the focus in which he keeps alive that sacred fire, which otherwise might escape from the face of the earth. Corruption of morals in the mass of cultivators is a phenomenon of which no age nor nation has furnished an example.[2]

Farmers would occupy territory and be hard-working and virtuous; they were also less susceptible to mobs and demagogues and therefore better guardians of republican government. In turn, republican government had a natural interest in promoting and protecting the independent, land-owning, republican farmer. The ills of France, Jefferson wrote from Paris in 1785, were the effect of bad government that put enormous wealth in the hands of a few proprietors and left the remaining nineteen million out of twenty million people "more wretched, more accursed in every circumstance of human existence than the most conspicuously wretched individual in the whole United States."[3] An "equal division of property is impracticable," he believed. But he still wanted "a little portion of land" owned by as many people as possible.[4] "...We have now lands enough to employ an infinite number of people in their cultivation."[5]

Such a faith in "the cultivators of the earth" is very easily ridiculed, and in our time many people have done so. It came from an intellectual gentleman whose own lands were cultivated by slaves, and he certainly did not call them "the chosen people of God." Moreover, Jefferson's opposition to manufacturing would have left the United States without any mines and factories, while his distrust of cities is often given as the source of American anti-urban feeling and our attraction today to suburbs, where 80 x 100-foot lots have become the modern citizen's "little portion of land." Jefferson was, in the fullest sense of the term, a pastoral sentimentalist, when "sentimentalism" was not yet a derogatory term. He believed in the superior benevolence, refinement, and honesty of the rural life, along with its power to teach thrift and self-discipline. Such a character was not incompatible with his rationalism. Better governments than those of Europe could be devised, he and his contemporaries believed. They need only be based on the wisdom of the most respected philosophers, ancient and modern, and most of them then located mankind's greatest happiness in the simple pastoral or agrarian life. That America was the place for such new beginnings both Europeans and Americans all agreed. So Jefferson had the support and respect of thousands of his fellow Americans, at least the free white males, rich and poor, in all sections of the country. Thus in 1784 the Continental Congress had made him the chair of a committee to plan for the government of the new "Western Territory"—or what is now Ohio, Indiana, Illinois, Michigan, and Wisconsin.

In his committee's first "Report," March 22, 1784, were recommendations on the size of new states, the procedures for admitting them into the United States, and the very significant resolution, "That after the year 1800 of the Christian era, there shall be neither slavery nor involuntary servitude in any of the said states."[6] This was a clear sign, as Lincoln later argued, that Jefferson did not want slavery to continue. By stopping its spread, Jefferson and other founding fathers expected it to decline and wither away. The West was to be free; and though that policy would later be challenged, first in the Missouri Compromise of 1819 and then in the debates over California statehood and the Nebraska Territory, it by and large held. The West not only was to be free, it was to become the hope of free people. It was there that many slaves fled and that many white Southerners also fled, escaping the unfair competition that slavery posed to free farmers and laborers. The "year 1800 of the Christian era" was still sixteen years away, and the Constitution of 1788 was a serious regression from the resolutions of 1784, but those resolutions had still taken a long step towards freedom. That too would affect the future landscape, as we will see later.

But the more immediate impact on the land of the Western Territory committee was through its "Ordinance establishing a Land Office for the United States," first introduced in Congress May 7, 1784. To obtain money with which to pay its debts, the new government needed to sell land, and to survey the land it "proposed to run straight north-south lines every tenth mile and to divide the Western Territory into squares of 100 geographical miles."[7] These two concepts, straight survey lines running north-south and east-west, and square lots, were the essence of the later Survey, even though the sizes of the divisions finally agreed upon were different. The basis of the proposal actually came from Hugh Williamson, a Pennsylvanian who had studied in Utrecht and admired the rectangular landscape of Holland, but Jefferson and other committee members all supported it. Their differences were simply over how large the lots should be. Jefferson, with his love of decimal systems, favored revision of the size of the acre so that there would be 1000 acres to the square mile, rather than 640, and there were other proposals affecting the size of grants to Revolutionary War veterans and the technicalities of survey methods.[8] Finally a new committee, chaired by William Grayson of Virginia, brought a revised Ordinance to Congress in April, 1785, and it was further revised and passed. It set the size of townships as six-miles square (which was deemed a more feasible governmental unit, being close to the size of townships in southern New England),[9] and ordered that a survey party of thirteen men (one from each state) was to begin "on the river Ohio at a point that shall be found to be due north from the western termination of a line, which has been run as the southern boundary of the state of Pennsylvania."[10] The head surveyor was then to run a line due west, on which marks on trees were to be made every mile and north-south lines or ranges run every six miles.

Accordingly, Thomas Hutchins, Geographer of the United States, began the Survey in late September, 1785, assisted by his deputy surveyors (only eight of the thirteen showed up), and thirty chain men, ax-men, and horse drivers. They started from the intersection of the Ohio River and the western border of Pennsylvania, which by then has been established, and Hutchins ran the latitudinal line west, which came to be known as "the Geographer's Line."[11] It became the base line, and from it seven longitudinal lines six miles apart were started south. But there were great difficulties. The eight surveyors had varied levels of experience and training. The land was hilly and forested, and there were many compass variations to contend with in distinguishing between magnetic north and true north. Danger from Indians was so great that forts were established to protect the surveyors–Fort Steuben at what is now Steubenville, Ohio, and Fort Harmar near Marietta. As a result, the work was poor and expensive, and after two years "only four ranges of townships were ready for sale." So the survey was discontinued. Nevertheless, the seven north-south or "range" lines were plotted, and the area is still known as "the Seven Ranges."[12]

To me that point at the intersection of the Pennsylvania-Ohio line and the Ohio River is an American "Greenwich Meridian." I know that in later years other baselines and "principal meridians" were selected, as more land became available for surveying and as fresh starts were made with newer equipment and techniques. The original Ohio territory itself was carved up into a number of different districts, such as the Ohio Company Purchase, the Virginia Military District, the Symes Purchase, the Connecticut Land Company, and the U.S. Military Reserve, and some of them were surveyed by different practices.[13] Ohio was like a survey testing ground, but the method that later prevailed, was basically the one started in the Seven Ranges area in 1785.

Therefore, on a recent trip back to Iowa from New York, my wife Hutha and I stopped in Steubenville to try to find that original point. I had not been in this little old steel town since I used to drive through it decades ago, when I had no idea that the whole West was, in a way, organized from here. Then it seemed only tough and dirty, and I had no desire to stop. But now we went to the public library to get advice, and from the way the staff helped us I felt as if we were back in smalltown Iowa. One person led us to another, and within an hour we were with Charlie Green, a local historian who had written a paper on the Seven Ranges and who told us to go up the Ohio River to

East Liverpool, where we would find a marker on the Ohio-Pennsylvania line.

So the next morning we drove out a worn two-lane road (Ohio 39) and found, in fact, three markers: one a stone obelisk dedicated September 30, 1960 by the East Liverpool Historical Society and the American Congress on Surveying and Mapping, the second an iron plaque put up by the Beaver County (Pennsylvania) Historical Research and Landmarks Foundation, and the third an iron plaque jointly sponsored by the East Liverpool, Columbiana County, and Ohio State historical societies and dated September 15, 1985. All agreed on the importance of the spot. Yet the obelisk and the Beaver Co. marker also said that the original point had really been 1112 feet to the south. So we tried to peer down through thick bushes and trees beside the road, but could see only railroad tracks, telephone poles, and a big warehouse. The obelisk had also been vandalized, and weeds and rubbish were everywhere. How revealing, I thought, that this little shrine honoring the place from which the survey of 70% of all American property began—our farms, homes, parks, businesses, everywhere we live and work—is itself in bad repair. Such is the condition of public spaces in a nation of individualism and private property.

But Hutha did not listen to my philosophizing. She wanted to get to that actual spot, 1112 feet to the south. So we drove back towards East Liverpool, crossed the train tracks, and parked in front of SH-BELL-CO – a company that stocks speciality materials for steel. The buildings looked run down, and I did not expect a kindly reception. Soon, however, Bob Galloway, the office manager, came out to the reception desk and gladly answered our questions. The location of the original marker, a stake placed by the surveyors of the Virginia (now West Virginia) and Pennsylvania border, had long ago been buried by thirty feet of slag from a steel mill that once was on this land. Additional slag had been dumped along the banks of the Ohio River. But about thirty or forty years ago the site had been excavated. He wasn't sure by whom or what had been found. Then it had been filled in again, and a building placed on top. He showed us the building on an aerial view hanging on the wall. People did occasionally come by, he said, and he seemed pleased to come tell what he knew. Like many Americans today, Galloway was very interested in his local history, yet a little surprised to find that others were interested too.

We drove back to Steubenville, looked briefly at the reconstruction of Fort Steuben (a hopeful sign of our emerging pride in local history), and then headed down the shore of the Ohio River. Our goal was Marietta, and as we drove we could easily see why Geographer Hutchins' surveyors had had such a hard time and why the roads of southeastern Ohio do not follow section lines! This is rough country – more like West Virginia and Kentucky – and must have been very rough country in 1785. It is not at all the Ohio I knew as a boy in Columbus. People in Columbus used to call people from southeastern Ohio hillbillies.

But Marietta, as the oldest Euro-American town

in Ohio, is an excellent place for studying the Seven Ranges. It lies just west of the southern tip of the seventh range, and the large museum, called Campus Martius, after the name of a fort that stood there, has a very informative exhibit of surveyors' tools and practices. Life-size figures dressed in nineteenth-century clothes hold up surveyors' chains and sticks, while the chief hunches behind a tripod and squints through his "circumferator," or surveyor's compass. The evolution of the circumferator is shown in a sequence of them made at different dates by one Alexander Platt of Columbus.

But the most instructive exhibit is one that is meant to illustrate the superiority of the rectangular survey to the metes and bounds surveys that had been used in the East and which were also used in the Virginia Military District, which lay between the Scioto River and the Little Miami River. In 1784, when Virginia and other states surrendered their claims to western land, Virginia had been allowed to retain this vast tract in order to satisfy warrants for free land that it had granted to its veterans. Since the tract lay in the western half of Ohio, that had not yet been surveyed, the holders of the warrants were allowed to go to the land, select what they liked, and make their own description of it, using as landmarks for the metes (or meeting points) and bounds (boundaries) natural features like rivers, creeks, and prominent trees. Then they took their descriptions to the land office, and hired their own surveyors to measure the area and make a more official description. This was filed, and they took title. But the results were chaotic. The earliest comers took the best land; their parcels were of all kinds of shapes; the sizes of the parcels could not be precisely determined; and in between these chosen parcels were both overlaps and "gores," or gaps, which led to later quarrels and lawsuits.

On one wall of this metes-and-bounds-vs.-rectangular-survey exhibit case are diagrams of some of the parcels in the Virginia Military District. They look like boomerangs, dragons, turtles, broken cookies, shattered glass, melted frypans with twisted handles, and other shapes indescribable – challenges to modern Chaos Theorists to measure and describe. There is also a modern aerial photograph of Circleville, Ohio, which lies on the Scioto River, south of Columbus, and thus on the border between the old Virginia Military District, to the west, and the land of the old U.S. Military Reserve, to the east, where the rectangular survey was used. Here, in one picture, is a contrast not just between two kinds of survey but between two worlds. Half the picture looks like the familiar American Middle West. The other half looks like Europe.[14] Surveying is not just a dull technical matter. How land is surveyed directly affects how land looks.

How it is surveyed also affects how it is bought and sold and how it is treated.

Despite all its apparent superiority to the metes and bounds practice, the rectangular survey was in a way fiendish. It rapidly converted the common land of Indians and trappers into private land and thus was an American equivalent of the infamous enclosure acts of

England and Scotland and Ireland that drove peasants out of their land and homes and turned the commons into private property. Metes and bounds surveys did this too, of course. But the rectangular survey did it more efficiently. It was a much more exact and reliable instrument. With good reason did American Indians sometimes harass the survey parties by pulling up their stakes and stealing their horses.

The extent to which the survey converted land into a commodity is illustrated in the sequence of laws that improved its methods and set the prices. Initially the lines were surveyed only every two miles, with posts placed halfway between them to designate individual miles and indicate corners of sections. This was a time-saver and was consistent with the early sale of land only in 640-acre sections. In 1800, in response to a demand for smaller parcels, some sections were divided and sold in 320-acre tracts. A few years later Albert Gallatin, Jefferson's Secretary of the Treasury, authorized sale in 160-acre tracts, with a price of $1.25 per acre for 640- and 320-acre parcels and $1.50 per acre for the 160-acre tracts. In 1820 the smallest unit was reduced to 80 acres, and in 1832 to 40 acres. In 1854 the "Graduation Act" reduced the price to $1.00 per acre for land that had been available for ten years or more, $.75 for land for sale for fifteen years, $.50 for land for sale for twenty years, $.25 for land for sale twenty-five years, and $.125 for land for sale for thirty years or more.[15] Such a price list gave no attention to the quality of the land –its contours, what was growing on it, where it was, or who had been living on it. In general, land that had not sold when first put on the market was hilly, swampy, or otherwise undesirable, but the Graduation Act established a clearance sale. Whatever the price, land could be bought, like cloth. The Homestead Act, making 160-acre parcels of government land free to people who would settle on it and improve it, was passed in 1862. But despite the Act's renewed emphasis on helping the Jeffersonian yeoman, it too treated land as a commodity.

The rectangular survey's accuracy and reliability further encouraged speculation. Surveyors were required by law to provide brief notes on the character of the land—whether it was hilly or flat, wet or dry, wooded or not—and this information, combined with the accurate measurement of the numbers of acres, facilitated the buying and selling of it, the way investors and speculators today buy, hold, and sell stocks. A distant uncle of mine in the 1840s, having prospered in banking in Lexington, Kentucky, bought hundreds of acres of Wisconsin land, sight unseen, and then sent some of the children of one of his less successful brothers out from New Jersey to manage it and eventually settle it.

The rectangular survey, of course, also established some completely unnatural borders. It was an abstract template that went down everywhere, regardless of rivers, lakes, forests, hills, marshes, and swamps. Never mind topography, the law said; just run straight lines. Thus today we have fences stretching precariously across creeks and even small rivers. We have the corners of four people's property meeting somewhere in the middle of a woods or wetland. And we have people trying to run fences along the sides of steep hills, where they are difficult to build and maintain and where it is also very difficult to extricate a stray cow or sheep.

Such straight lines were the instruments of quantification, and quantification, too, has had many consequences on our land and life. Land that is numerically measured to the fraction of an acre is easy to tax and to mortgage, which, in turn, facilitates banking and governing. It is also easy to evaluate in terms of its productivity. The emphasis throughout the cornbelt and wheatbelts on yields per acre would be impossible were it not so easy to determine, first of all, exactly how big a field is. Fields with curving or waving or diagonal boundaries are not nearly so readily measured. Quantifiable land lends itself inevitably to quantifiable, commodity agriculture.

In turn, straight lines, right angles, and precisely measured fields have contributed to mechanized agriculture. A giant plow or combine moves much more easily in a long, straight line than along a property line that turns and twists. Thus, the rectangular survey quietly underlies American agriculture's ever-developing farm machinery. A farmer goes into his field and proceeds to plow along the fence line, turn, and run the next pass parallel to the first, and so on. A few weeks later, he plants his crop along the same lines. In early summer he cultivates between the rows he has planted. And in the fall his combine moves down the same rows. This promotes efficiency, but it also promotes soil compaction. The weight of the heavy tractors and equipment pressing down in the same rows time after time squeezes the particles of soil together, making it harder for the soil to absorb water and air and harder for roots to grow.

Another disadvantage to plowing and planting parallel to fence lines is that it promotes erosion, because it does not observe the contour of the land. The tilted furrows between the rows readily become trenches and gullies down which water pours, taking soil with it. Ironically, Jefferson himself had noted this, as had other thoughtful agriculturists back to Roman times, and had laid guidelines in his fields so that plows wound around the hillsides, leaving rows and furrows that ran perpendicular to their slopes.[16] But the mass of American frontier farmers did not do the same. They took pride in being able to plow a straight furrow. It was a virtue, which fathers tried to pass on to sons, the father critically watching the sons and the sons nervously seeking approval. County plowing contests also rewarded farmers for fast, straight work. All across the country, farmers young and old competed at it. It was another virtue to have long, straight, weed-free rows of corn, or whatever other grain you grew. You and your neighbors all knew it, and judged each other accordingly, as suburbanites today judge each other by their straight-cut lawns. But the badly cut lawn can be recut a week later, whereas a crooked field of corn is there all summer, as embarrassing to a farmer as a mess of typos is to an author or editor. Jefferson, the Survey, and the Grid are not directly responsible for such values—perhaps Jefferson least of all. But the Grid still underlay them. It was like the page on which the lines and margins were drawn.

Thus it was not until the intervention of the federal government's Soil Conservation Service, a New-Deal agency of the 1930s and '40s, that large numbers of farmers on rolling land began to contour plow. The SCS made it a condition of government grants and subsidies. Terracing was another government-encouraged practice that broke up the straight lines, as did "strip farming" (planting different crops in adjacent bands 50-75 feet wide) and leaving the "water courses" of a field in twisting bands of grass.[17]

An even more severe effect of the Grid, however, has been the rerouting of the streams that naturally drain a field. The contour of a field is changed so as to make it more even or regular. The drainage is directed so as to minimize its disruption to plowing. Finally, the nearby streams themselves may be rechanneled so that they run in straight lines along the field's edge. The result is a field with ditches beside it that looks like an irrigated field in California, except that the water in these ditches is not being brought to the field; it is being carried away. What such fields further have in common, though, is that they are usually large and are part of an operation (so-called) that is more like a factory than a farm. Its primary standards are making money—as much a possible, as rapidly as possible.

But the big combines, contour farming, stream-diversions, and giant fields have been twentieth-century developments. At first the surveyors' carefully drawn lines were barely visible. They were, as John Mack Faragher says, just a "geometric template [that] lay dormant, to awaken fully only with the stirrings of rural commercial development."[18] The first fields were only a few acres, surrounded by zigzag split-rail fences, and with tree-stumps still standing in them. The Iowa writer Herbert Quick remembered that out on the prairies when he was a boy in the 1860s "the landscape was a glorious undulating sea of waving prairie grass, on which floated here and there a quadrangular raft of tillage. The roads were wagon tracks, running diagonally from the villages to the farms, and in main roads from town to town." It was only with the increase in tilled fields that the roads were forced off what Quick called "their antigodlin courses" and straightened out into the alleyways along the section lines.[19] Even then the straight roads were but faint and narrow, just wagon tracks between fences, fences that themselves did not become straight and strong until the introduction of barbed wire in the 1870s. From then on, wire fences also made the marking and maintaining of property lines easier. At the section edges, the right of way for roads was designated in most states and counties as thirty-three feet (half a chain, with each landowner giving up a rod or 16 ½ feet of property), but the rule was not always closely followed, and until recently the road itself was ungraded and unpaved.

Could one have had aerial view of Illinois, Iowa, or eastern Nebraska in 1900 one would have seen many more and smaller farms, with smaller fields growing a much greater variety of crops. Thus the "geometric template" of the survey would have been harder to see, hidden between the many little squares and rectangles, and not so neatly and visibly ruled off by the county roads. It was the automobile's needs that brought in gravel in the 1920s, making white lines on the green or brown or black background of the fields. Then it was high-powered road graders in the 1950s and '60s that crowned these gravel roads, deepened the ditches beside them, and made them more level. At the same time, farm consolidation and monocropping smoothed out the small patchwork fields of 80 and 40 acres and less into the bigger fields that are so visible from an airplane today.

Now, finally, the simple, geometric template is most boldly seen. Fields are 320 and 640 acres, and all in one crop, as passengers flying over in jets seven miles up can easily observe. These massive fields are black or brown in the spring, just before planting. Narrow rows of green appear against the black as the corps emerge in early June. In summer comes a brilliant array of greens in almost every section, edge to edge, road to road. In fall the combines go out and peel off strip after strip of the golden ripe crops, until the fields are brown or black again.

But as the symmetry of the Grid has become more distinct, the Jeffersonian pastoral ideology has become fainter, and maybe even forgotten. Back in the years between 1910 and 1920, when the fields and farms were small, there were roughly 32 million American farmers. In 1950 there were still 23 million farmers, and on a square mile of farmland in Illinois or Iowa there still might be four farms. An average of four farms per section meant that a township, with maybe 32 sections farmed and the rest used for towns, schools, and a park, could have a thousand people in it, a viable political unit. By 1991 the farm population was down to just 4.6 million, so low that in 1993 the U.S. Census Bureau announced it would "no longer count the number of Americans who live on farms."[20] The Jeffersonian "cultivators of the soil" are so few and insignificant that our government counts them no more! The chosen people of God are presumably gone, and with them the rural communities that they shopped in, went to school in, and voted in.

For me to appreciate all these changes in the prairie landscape and understand their relation to such a simple but universal influence as the rectangular survey has taken many years. Although the Grid is now more visible than ever before and, thanks to jet planes, visible to more people than ever before, its history is probably less known, just as the land itself is less clearly seen. The perspective from seven miles up can be grand and breathtaking, or it can seem monotonous, but in either case, it is only one perspective. Likewise the perspective from an Interstate Highway, smooths out the ups and downs of the rolling prairie and misses the small towns, with closed up stores, and empty Main Streets.

The Interstates, meanwhile, are one of the forces that are challenging the rectangular survey. As Don

Worster noted several years ago in writing about the prairie photographs of Terry Evans, some human forces in the landscape have always been opposed to the governmental rigidity of the grid.[21] The railroads almost never followed section lines, because they had to submit to topography and also sought to go directly between cities. Now Interstates and other modern highways often have been built on diagonals, despite the protests of farmers. In Iowa, two such protests are legendary. The first, many years ago, came with the building of U.S. 65 on a northeast diagonal from Des Moines to Marshalltown. Farmers along the route accused the highway department of slicing through their fields; and newspapers in Marshalltown and other smaller towns cried out that it was a conspiracy organized by the Des Moines Register in order to speed delivery of the Register and take business away from local papers, while drawing shoppers into Des Moines. Similar outcries came with the building of I-380 on a diagonal between Cedar Rapids and Waterloo.

Such protests have helped confirm the idea that Midwesterners love squares and hate diagonals and curves. But pipelines and powerlines are also cutting across the fields and forcing realignments, and it is conceivable that such lines will eventually become legal boundaries, dividing our fields into new shapes. Another force, that could become ever more decisive, is the Federal Natural Resource Conservation Service's programs for taking some land out of production, especially highly erodible land, riparian land, and wetlands, and planting it in native plants and grasses for long periods of time. Acreages thus set aside are not generally rectangular. They therefore break the checkerboard symmetry, and the fields they break into are often replanted in different patterns, following contours and being planted in strips of different crops.

These forces are not going to take us back to a metes and bounds survey. They will impose new systems on top of the old rectangular survey. But I like them, generally, because they promise to bring us not only a more interesting landscape but also one that is more reflective of the courses of rivers, the slopes of hills, and the land as it once was. I have also grown to like many things about the Grid. I appreciate the Jeffersonian rationalism which is responsible for its simplicity and uniformity. I have gotten to depend on straight north-south and east-west roads in finding my way in and out of Midwestern towns, even though I take diagonals when I can. And I like the straight and four-square character that seems to be derived, in part, from this geometry. Such virtues seem related, as well, to Jeffersonian agrarianism – to independence, a love of space and freedom, a respect for others, and a lack of cunning. I do not go along with attacks on Jefferson as a naïve, arrogant, and elitist philosopher who could "sit at a drawing table in one's library and deduce the nature of the world."[22] The legacy of Jefferson and the Northwest Territory Ordinance, both politically and geographically, is one that people living today in the prairies, as well as the old Northwest, should cherish and be proud of. Our job is to add to it the lessons of ecology and soil conservation, so that we can have a landscape that also, in Aldo Leopold's words preserves the "integrity, stability, and beauty of the biotic community."[23] That's the place that I am working for and where I want to live.

Notes:

1Hildegard Binder Johnson, Order Upon the Land: The U.S. Rectangualr Land Survey and the Upper Mississippi Country (New York:Oxford Univ. Press, 1976), Preface.

2 Thomas Jefferson, Notes on the State of Virginia, ed. William Peden (New York: W.W. Norton, 1954), pp. 164-5.

3 Thomas Jefferson, The Life and Selected Writings of..., ed. Adrienne Koch & William Peden (New York: Modern Library, 1944), p. 372.

4 Jefferson, Life…, pp. 389-90.

5Jefferson, Life..., p. 377 (Letter to John Jay, Paris, August 23, 1785).

6 Jefferson, Life..., pp. 314-5.

7 Johnson, p. 42

8 Johnson, p. 42.

9 Johnson, p. 44.

10"Land Ordinance of 1785," in C. Albert White, A History of the Rectangular Survey (U.S. Department of the Interior, 1983), p. 12.

11 William Donohue Ellis, The Ordinance of 1787: The Nation Begins (Dayton, Ohio: Landfall Press, 1987), p. 55.

12 Johnson, p. 48.

13 White, A History..., pp. 24-45.

14 An extreme example of the inaccuracies of the metes and bounds survey is given in The History of the Rectangular Survey. A parcel in Scioto County (in the Virginia Military District) was originally recorded as containing 458.5 acres, but when it was resurveyed in 1925, it was found to have 1,662 acres. See White, p. 28.

15 This brief account of survey legislation is taken from Johnson, pp. 55-65.

16 Johnson, p. 196.

17 Johnson, pp. 193-204.

18 Faragher, Sugar Creek: Life on the Illinois Prairie (Yale Univ. Press, 1986), p. 43.

19 Herbert Quick, One Man's Life (Indianapolis: Bobbs Merrill Co., 1925), p. 191. Willa Cather describes the same changes in My Antonia.

20 Wendell Berry, Another Turn of the Crank (Washington DC: Counterpoint, 1995), p. 8. Berry quotes from a New York Times article in October, 1993.

21 Donald Worster, "A Tapestry of Change: Nature and Culture on the Prairie," in Terry Evans, The Inhabited Prairie (Lawrence, KS: University Press of Kansas, 1998), pp.xv-xvi.

22 Richard Manning, Grassland: The History, Biology, Politics, and Promise of the American Prairie (New York: Viking, 1995), p. 95.

23 Aldo Leopold, A Sand County Almanac (New York: Ballantine Books, 1966), p. 262.

NOT SO PLAIN: ART OF THE AMERICAN PRAIRIES

Joni L. Kinsey

Since the first European encounters with the grasslands of central North America, beginning with Coronado in the mid-sixteenth century, prairies have alternately confused, dismayed, overwhelmed, depressed, and inspired those who would contend with their contradictions.[1] They have been described as being both nothing and everything, empty as well as vast, monotonous and endlessly varied. For those who saw them in their pristine state, prairies were often disorienting and a place to be lost, whereas today they have become the "heartland" where Americans look to find their truest identity. While such disparities have frustrated many who have attempted to convey something of this landscape to others, visual artists, perhaps even more than writers, have encountered special difficulties, primarily because of the prairie's lack of geographical features that would contribute to a "view."[2] The European conventions of composing landscape images that dominated painting until the twentieth century were completely unsuited to such a featureless country, and the metaphorical alternatives available to literary portrayers were, for the most part, non-visual. As a result, many artists avoided the subject, even those who were committed to documenting their experiences and who in their travels encountered the scenery daily for long periods. The solutions of others were more enterprising, however, both in the nineteenth century and more recently. Although their art has been overshadowed by other types of landscapes, grassland pictures constitute a significant genre within American art that is as subtle, challenging, and fascinating as the land and the history it depicts.[3]

Prairies and visual depictions of them are misunderstood or underappreciated for a variety of reasons, both cultural and aesthetic. A frequent complaint is that they appear too simple, too monotonous, and, befitting their name, too plain. The land lacks the pastoral tranquility of eastern landscapes and the drama of far western ones; its most consistent feature, at least before cultivation, was flat or gently rolling terrain and endless grass, only rarely punctuated by sloughs, draws, and the all too infrequent wooded creek beds and river bottoms. As botanists, geographers, historians, and geologists are well aware, however, the prairies and plains are actually highly complex in virtually every way—ecologically, historically, and metaphorically. Even the most superficial attempts to discuss them requires labyrinthian negotiation of shifting locations, grassland types, and varying species of plants, annual rainfall, and longitudinal orientation, not to mention the maze of associations that have shaped our cultural understanding of this most perplexing of regions.[4] What appears monolithic from a distance is, upon closer scrutiny, almost infinitely varied. Indeed, the prairie's most consistent characteristic may be that of a paradox between appearance and actuality, idea and fact. In direct contrast to its initial impression, the prairie offers an artistic paradigm of sublime proportions: the significance of the subject is equalled only by the struggle to express it.

With the possible exception of seascapes to which it was often likened, the utter starkness of the grasslands was unprecedented for most early viewers. As the late nineteenth-century Canadian painter Edward Roper joked, "There's a good deal more scenery wanted in this country, ain't there."[5]Until modernist aesthetics validated minimalism in the mid-twentieth century, many artists despaired of portraying the landscape without something—anything—to provide depth, a sense of scale, variety, and meaning in their pictures. Although a number of them described a variety of reactions to the emptiness, including emotions associated with the romantic sublime (awe, fear, and delight to name only a few), rarely did nineteenth-century artists translate these into images that might correspond with European art of the sublime, such as the paintings of the English painter Joseph Mallord William Turner or the German artist, Caspar David Friederich.[6]

Writers also struggled to express their awe of the unbroken expanse, but even when they felt their words inadequate they could always resort to classic metaphors such as "oceans of grass," which transform the prairie into something else, but at least by association convey a mental image of uninterrupted horizons. And writers can abstract ideas in clarifying ways, a tactic virtually unavailable to visual artists. Especially evocative in this regard is Willa Cather's characterization from My Antonia, "There was nothing but land: not a country at all, but the material out of which countries are made."[7] In this perceptive statement, Cather expresses a common theme, the potential of prairies, by explaining what they are through the prospect of what they can be.

The prairie's prospects were also a central theme of painters and photographers, but since they were unable to utilize the writer's metaphors, and the prevailing visual and aesthetic models concerned landscapes of very different sorts, artists were forced either to invent new visual strategies or adapt existing ones. At the same time, their work was complicated by the multiple connotations the issue of prospect had within the visual tradition and the profound implications these had when applied to prairie landscapes. "Prospect" in the art world referred, in various contexts, to the point of view which is fundamental to visual representation, the vantage point which was often literally a promontory overlooking a scene, the scene itself, the elevation that would render such a vista accessible, the ownership which was central to the meaning of eighteenth-century estate portraits known as "Prospect paintings," and finally, a looking forward in time, a futurity that was suggested by the view toward the horizon. It is the multivalent exploration of the prairie's "prospects" that makes the art of the region so significant, aesthetically and culturally.[8]

The "empty" grasslands did not, of course, offer many prospects in any sense of the term.[9] They seemed an almost sublime void that both compelled and defied representation or appropriation. Artists responded in two basic ways: they either avoided depicting prairies altogether or they took great care to include something that would provide the prairies with prospects of some sort. Solutions were contrived from what was at hand or they were imported; ridges, hillocks, river bluffs, and (later) windmills served as vantage points, wagons, sod houses, or Native American dwellings offered a sense of scale, and native fauna and eventually gardens, orchards, and cropland suggested abundance and potential.

Such constructions of visual interest not only served an artistic function, however, satisfying the conventions of landscape painting, they also paralleled the EuroAmerican development of the prairies themselves. Just as Americans transformed the actual grasslands according to their needs, preconceptions, and ideals, filling them first with small inroads of survey parties and scattered settlements and then with trees, section lines, large-scale agriculture, and superhighways, so too did artists construct their views of prairies. Their inclusions and manipulations form a metaphorical taxonomy of the landscape's conceptual and physical transformation, but more than mere reflectors of cultural change, the images embody the aesthetic reconciliations that made those changes possible. In other words, the images document the psychological adjustments to the terrain that were necessary not only for artists, but for any who would confront the prairie landscape and attempt to conform it to their purposes.[10]

These reconciliations, in the form of practical solutions to the visual void of the prairies, are apparent in the earliest depictions of the region by Titian Peale (ca. 1799-1885) and Samuel Seymour (ca. 1775-after 1823) who traveled with the government-sponsored Long expedition in 1819-20.[11] Better known, however, are George Catlin, Karl Bodmer, and Alfred Jacob Miller, all of whom encountered but rarely depicted vacant prairies in their private travels during the 1830s. Even Catlin (1896-1872), who did paint a few panels that contain little more than blue and green bands, usually included Native Americans, bison, or events such as fire, or he focused on the few prairie landforms such as the Loess Hills in present-day western Iowa to relieve the visual monotony (fig. 1). He was, of course, most interested in the lives of the native peoples, having taken on the cause of becoming their champion, but his response to the landscape as described in his writings suggests additional reasons he avoided painting the empty grassland. Occasionally Catlin remarked on the "allurements" of the "splendid panorama," but more often noted the gloom of silence and the tortuous sameness.[12]

Fig. 1 Catlin, George (1896-1872)
Beautiful Prairie Bluffs, Upper Missouri, 1835-36
oil on canvas, 19 ½ x 27 ½"
Smithsonian American Art Museum, Washington, D.C.,
Gift of Mrs. Joseph Harrison, Jr.. (1985.66.329)

At the same time as he was overwhelmed with the disparity of human and geographical scale, echoing the feelings of many explorers and settlers who found themselves apparently lost within the expanse, Catlin also, however, envisioned a prospect for the prairies that eluded others. As an alternative to the annihilation he foresaw for the native people and animals of the plains as whites encroached on their territory, he proposed "a nation's park" that would preserve their way of life. This was practical, he argued, since "this strip of country, which extends from the province of Mexico to Lake Winnipeg on the North, is almost one entire plain of grass...[and] is, and ever must be, useless to cultivating man."[13] The first to conceive the national park idea, Catlin was ahead of his time by nearly forty years (Yellowstone was designated the first national park in 1872), and even though he regarded the plains as "uniformly sterile," he would surely be today among the forefront of the prairie preservation movement that is still working to institute his idea, albeit without the same emphasis on the human inhabitants and with a very different appreciation for the landscape itself.

By contrast, Catlin's contemporary Karl Bodmer (1809-1893), a Swiss artist who had been thoroughly indoctrinated into the conventions of landscape painting, virtually ignored the prairie landscape. Even though he painted numerous, exquisite views of rivers and spent considerable time inland during his travels with Prince Maximillian of Wied in 1833-34, his closest subject to prairies was Mandan Shrine (fig. 2) in which he carefully foregrounded the ritual objects that were

Fig. 2. Bodmer, Karl (1809-1893)
Mandan Shrine, 1833, watercolor on paper, 8 x 10 3/8"
Joslyn Art Museum, Omaha (1986.49.168)

for him the subject of the work. Alfred Jacob Miller (1810-1874), who traveled through much of the same country a few years later with the Scottish nobleman Sir William Drummond Stewart and was hired to produce souvenirs of the excursion, also took care to focus on dramatic action or evocative themes.[14] In works such as The Lost Greenhorn (Buffalo Bill Historical Center, Cody, Wyoming), for example, Miller represented a continual fear among prairie travelers in the form of a forlorn figure who searches desperately and vainly for landmarks that might locate him amid the waving grass.[15] His Prairie Scene: Mirage (1858-60, Walters Art Gallery, Baltimore) also embodies a common effect of the shimmering grassland and is reminiscent of Catlin's description:

> *One commences on peregrinations like these, with a light heart, and a nimble foot, and spirit is as buoyant as the very air that floats along by the side of him; but his spirit soon tires, and he lags on the way that is rendered more tedious and intolerable by the tantalizing mirage that opens before him beautiful lakes, and lawns and copses; or by the looming of the prairie ahead of him, that seems to rise like a parapet, and decked with its varied flowers, phantom-like, flies and moves along before him...*[16]

For artists who followed this first generation of EuroAmerican portrayers, the challenge of the landscape's emptiness remained, but because of a variety of cultural and technological developments that were beginning to open the region to white settlement and commercial development, the prairie's prospects were beginning to improve, literally and figuratively. Furthermore, artists became more adept at utilizing indigenous features in creative ways and were less hampered by artistic conventions since landscape paintings, especially exotic or unusual ones, had become more acceptable in the United States since the 1830s.[17] William Jacob Hays (1830-1875), who traveled up the Missouri River in 1860, was a particularly inventive portrayer with his views of bison

Fig 3. Hays, William Jacob (1830-1875)
A Herd of Buffaloes on the Bed of the River Missouri
[*Herd On the Move*], ca. 1860-62, oil on canvas, 36 x 72",
Thomas Gilcrease Institute of American History and Art, Tulsa, Oklahoma (0137.533)

(fig. 3) in which the animals pour down from the ridges, becoming the rivers and monumental features that the land lacked. Not content with the limitations of a single canvas to convey the power of such a scene, Hays made this large painting the central image of a triptych, a three-panel form historically associated with highly significant subjects.[18] United, the paintings embody the prodigiousness of prairies and place the subject among the pantheon of artistic hierarchy.

Expeditions also offered substantial material for filling visual compositions. The winding wagon trains and pack animals could substitute for the meandering paths and streams of more conventional landscapes (as in William Henry Jackson's California Crossing, South Platte, 1867, Gilcrease Museum, Tulsa), or if standing still the horses and figures stood in place of trees and rocks (e.g. William Ranney's Halt on the Prairie, 1850, Huntington Art Gallery, Austin, Texas). Beyond the formal contribution to the pictures' interest, however, the "prospecting" or investigatory mission of expeditions was undoubtedly an implied component of their usefulness to artists as they sought to instill a notion of futurity to their images.

Even the prospect of death provided subject matter that would, ironically, enliven prairie pictures. On his 1866 journey through the West with General John Pope, Worthington Whittredge (1820-1910) found graves near Kearney, Nebraska to fill the foreground of a view (fig. 4), and throughout the nineteenth century and even today similarly stark

Fig 4. Whittredge, Thomas Worthington (1820-1910) Graves of Travellers Fort Kearney, Nebraska, 1866, oil on paper on canvas, 18.8 x 56.5 cm., Cleveland Museum of Art, Andrew R. and Martha Holden Jennings Fund, 1969.19

nineteenth century and even today similarly stark memento mori poignantly evoke the desolation of the prairie for those who experienced it before us. Whittredge traveled west again in 1870 in the company of fellow artists John Kensett and Sanford Gifford, and although these men were also accomplished landscapists, of the group only Whittredge, who is better known for his scenes of dense forests in Pennsylvania, produced many images of the prairie. In contrast to others who found the grasslands oppressive, he wrote later in his autobiography of his awe of the limitless horizons:

> *I had never seen the plains or anything like them. They impressed me deeply. I cared more for them than for the mountains, and very few of my western pictures have been produced from sketches made in the mountains, but rather from those made on the plains and with the mountains in the distance. Whoever crossed the plains at that period, notwithstanding its herds of buffalo and flocks of antelope, its wild horses, deer and fleet rabbits, could hardly fail to be impressed with its vastness and silence and the appearance everywhere of an innocent, primitive existence.*[19]

Later in his autobiography Whittredge said of the "vastness and impressiveness of the plains," that "nothing could be more like an Arcadian landscape."[20] Even though the artist usually took care to include the defining elements of mountains in his plain pictures, in this view the prospect of his prairie as an ambiguous place of death and dislocation was coupled with another, one that still influences our understanding of the region—a virginal paradise that even with its emptiness could suggest a prelapsarian garden.

Garden of Eden associations had been central to a mythic America since Columbus's arrival and continued unabated through the nineteenth century, but Whittredge notwithstanding, these metaphors became problematic in the context of the early prairies.[21] Landscapes of a more arcadian sort better served the Adamic myth, and it was only after the arrival of technology that facilitated agriculture—in the form of barbed wire, windmills, sodbreaking plows, and railroads that began in earnest in the 1870s—that the garden image could be applied to the treeless plains.[22] As Henry Nash Smith has explained, with the influx of optimistic settlers claiming and cultivating land, the enthusiastic promotions of the government, railroads, and other corporations intent on increasing commerce, and the post-Civil War enthusiasm for westward expansion, "it was therefore necessary that the settler's battle with drought and dust and wind and grasshoppers should be supported by the westward extension of the myth of the garden."[23] That the myth bordered on tall tale seemed irrelevant; Colorado Governor William Gilpin, geologist Ferdinand Hayden, journalist Horace Greeley and others steadfastly claimed that "rain followed the plow," and that the grasslands would, in time and with careful cultivation, become a blooming garden.[24]

The arcadian view did not completely displace the earlier, more elemental one, but rather alternated with it, as it does in life on the plains, according to fluctuations in the weather, economy and politics.

Fig. 5 Cover, Sallie (active 1880s-90s)
Homestead of Ellsworth Ball, Nebraska,
1880s oil on canvas, 19 1/2 x 23"
Nebraska State Historical Society, Lincoln

Thus we can have contrasts such as Sallie Cover's which epitomizes the prairie-as-garden metaphor, and Imogene See's more desolate view, Nebraska Farmstead (1880s, Joslyn Museum of Art, Omaha) from about the same time. Neither of these women artists is known other than from these single pictures, and it is presumed that they were themselves homesteader's wives, who, like Abby in Bess Streeter Aldrich's Nebraska novel, A Lantern in Her Hand (1928), sought cultivation of their own sort by taking brush in hand and painting the world around them.[25]

The lives of women in the plains region have been portrayed by diarists, historians, and artists primarily as one of drudgery, filth, and loneliness, and this is clearly portrayed both in photographs and in paintings, such as Harvey Dunn's Homesteader's Wife (1920s, South Dakota Museum of Art, Brookings).[26] But women were also depicted as graces of the prairie, civilizing muses who brought both heroism and even sophistication to the place. Most successful of these views are those that present such figures in the landscape. Through immersion the figures become striking by contrast to the landscape and at the same time united with the land through their common elemental passions. From these representations it is only a small step to presenting women as symbols of fertility and abundance that echo that of the land itself, as in Dunn's The Prairie is My Garden (1950, South Dakota Museum of Art, Brookings).

The most pointed use of such gendered symbolism, however, and one that is highly ironic, is Mother Earth Laid Bare (1938, fig. 6) by the

Fig 6. Hogue, Alexandre (1898-1994), Erosion No. 2 Mother Earth Laid Bare, 1936, oil on canvas, 44 x 56", Philbrook Museum of Art, Tulsa, Oklahoma (Museum purchase, 1946.4)

Fig 7. Wood, Grant (1891-1942), Fall Plowing, 1931, oil on canvas, 30 x 40 3/4", John Deere Collection, Moline, Ilinois

Texas/Oklahoma artist Alexandre Hogue (1898-1994), especially when it is compared to Grant Wood's bucolic Iowa scene, Fall Plowing (1931, fig. 7).[27] Like Annette Kolodny's book, The Lay of the Land (1975) which played off Henry Nash Smith's earlier title, Virgin Land (1950), Hogue's symbolic depiction of the eroded landscape relies not only on our recognizing the Depression era drought that turned the western plains into the Dust Bowl, but also on our understanding the implications of a raped Mother Earth, laid bare by man.[28] That the man, at least if we see the painting through the foil of Wood's picture, is John Deere, whose sodbreaking plow enabled the plains to be settled, is ironic since the painting today is owned by the Deere Corporation.[29] Wood's painting depicts a shining, new Deere-style plow (although a virtual anachronism by 1931) in the same position as the broken one in Hogue's. In Hogue's devastated scene, instead of bringing rain and redemption to a mythic land, the plow brings hardship and humiliation, hunger and heartache, fulfilling the early prophecy that the land was unfit for cultivation, only now it was cultivation itself that had rendered it so.

Following the New Deal era which focused tremendous attention on regional landscapes including those of the prairie/plains region, modernist abstraction in the 1950s through the 1970s virtually ignored landscape subjects. It has reemerged recently, however, with a strength recalling the nineteenth century, and prairiescapes of all sorts are receiving new attention, not only by Westerners with whom they have long been popular, but as well by east coast dealers, critics, and scholars. In some ways, the art world has finally grown into the subject, and as contemporary Americans struggle ever more vainly to locate themselves within an increasingly complex society, prairies have become a focal point for cultural identification, reflecting back to us our most cherished ideals of harmony with the land, and for those with more fortitude, pragmatism, or insight, our vainest follies and tragic mistakes.

Today a growing group of artists, such as Harold Gregor, James Winn, Terry Evans, Genie Patrick, and Keith Jacobshagen, to name just a few, are turning to the prairies for inspiration (fig. 8). In their hands, with the perspective of twentieth-century developments in art, land use, and technology,

Fig 8. Patrick, Genie (b. 1938)
A Season Turning, 1994
Oil on canvas, 47" x 80"
Collection of the artist, Iowa City
Photograph by David Trawick

we encounter a very different place than did the nineteenth-century visitors and settlers. The contemporary prairie has been transformed, to the point of having what might be thought of as almost too many prospects. The land has been filled and altered to the point of losing its identity; instead of looking in vain for something to break the expanse as our predecessors did, we must search for the uninterrupted view. It is as well a contested landscape, with competing forces—from environmentalists to agribusiness people, industrialists to suburban dwellers—vying for the prairie's future, and except in times of natural catastrophe such as tornadoes, droughts, or floods, it seems as if humans have gained the upper hand.

Today's grasslands, to borrow from the name of the southwestern Illinois landscape Charles Dickens visited in the 1840s, are "Looking-Glass Prairies."[30]

The prairie is no longer alien or forbidding, indeed it is mostly as manicured, trimmed, combed, and accessorized as we are ourselves. Fulfilling the desires of the nineteenth-century artists and settlers, the actual landscape has been framed and endowed with all manner of cultivations, and we must look closely for its original characteristics just as aging faces strain for vestiges of youth when confronted with a mirror. At the same time, the prairies reflect our cultural uncertainties and disagreements as they form the locus for continual debates over land use and its meaning. Like figures in the tall grass of the virgin prairie, the grasslands within contemporary society throw both the elemental and the human into high relief, each revealed by the character of the other.

For artists the competing prospects and challenges of the modern prairie are no less compelling. Instead of relying solely on the traditional linear perspective that characterized earlier landscape views, artists now present the region from a wide variety of angles—looking down from airplanes, from within the land itself as it becomes a sculptural form of its own (as in the remarkable crop art of Kansan Stan Herd), and sometimes with ambiguous points of view, as if we are floating tenuously between earth and sky, as in many of Keith Jacobshagen's spectacular paintings. The old notion of prospect, that of the vantage point, has finally been successfully commingled with its other connotation—that of possibility—as the artist mediates the prairie's multivalent relevance to contemporary culture.

Throughout it all, in the midst of competing visions and though transformed from their original state, the grass and the horizon retain their power, and as the contemporary prairie artists show us, we are made more significant by our relationship with them. As writer Theodore Winthrop put it in the 1860s:

> *Breadth of thought they claim, these dwellers on the sweeping prairies, a wide worldly range and terrestrial stride of seven leagues...their landscape is all horizon—limitless, oceanlike, with no pyramid mountain monuments of deathless heavens that are above the earth. In prairieland thought may go galloping onward unchecked, saying this I will locate...*[31]

It seems that location is what prairies and their representations are really about. At the same time as they disorient us, dislocating us from familiar references and reliable features, they offer us a prospect that confronts us with our own true nature.

NOTES

This article is a slightly modified reprint of an article first published in *Great Plains Quarterly 15* (Summer 1995): 185-200. For a more extensive treatment of the subject see my book, Plain Pictures: Images of the American Prairie (Washington, D.C.: Smithsonian Institution Press, 1996).

1. Francisco Vsquez de Coronado was the first European explorer of the plains in 1541. See George P. Hammond and Agapito Rey, eds., Narratives of the Coronado Expedition, 1540-1542 (Albuquerque: The Quivira Society, 1940).

2. For more on the literary treatment of the prairies see Robert Thacker, The Great Prairie Fact and Literary Imagination (Albuquerque: University of New Mexico Press, 1989).

3. While landscape art of other American regions has received extensive attention in major exhibitions, books, and scholarly articles, prairie painting has been discussed only within discussions of western art more generally or in scattered articles. Some of these include Roger B. Stein, "Packaging the Great Plains: The Role of the Visual Arts," Great Plains Quarterly 5 (Winter 1985): 5-23; Howard Lamar, "Seeing More than Earth and Sky: The Rise of a Great Plains Aesthetic," Great Plains Quarterly 9 (Spring 1989): 69-77; and idem., "Image and Counterimage: The Regional Artist and the Great Plains Landscape," in The Big Empty: Essays on Western Landscapes As Narrative, ed. Leonard Engel (Albuquerque: University of New Mexico Press, 1994), pp. 75-92.

4. While recognizing the many different characteristics and designations of prairie types (such as tallgrass, short grass, mixed grass, and high plains) and the geographical distinctions between prairie and plains terrain, in this study I am using the terms "plains" and "prairies" interchangeably. While scientifically incorrect, this commingling is consistent with both nineteenth-century and twentieth-century common usage referring to the grasslands of central North America.

5. Edward Roper, By Track and Trail Through Canada London: W.H. Allen, 1891), 51, cited in Ronald Rees, "Painting, Place, and Identity: A Prairie View," Environmental Aesthetics: Essays in Interpretation, edited by Barry Sadler, and Allen Carlson (Victoria: University of Victoria, 1982), pp. 117-141.

6. A thorough discussion of this complex aesthetic and its relation to prairie landscapes and their portrayers lies beyond the scope of this short essay, but it seems clear than at least some of the artists of the prairie were familiar with European aesthetic theory, including the sublime, which was a frequent topic of art critics in journals such as The Crayon, or later The Aldine. See also my Plain Pictures, especially chapter 1 (pp. 11-31).

7. Willa Cather, My Antonia (1918) repr. ed. (Boston: Houghton Mifflin Co, 1977), p. 7.

8. Definitions adapted from the Oxford English Dictionary, 1971, s.v. prospects. For more on prospect painting and related issues see Stephen Daniels, "Goodly Prospects: English Estate Portraiture, 1670-1730," in Mapping the Landscape: Essays on Art and Cartography, edited by Nicholas Alfrey and Stephen Daniels (Nottingham: University Art Gallery, Castle Museum, 1990), pp. 9-17; and Albert Boime, The Magisterial Gaze: American Landscape Painting, 1830-1865 (Washington: Smithsonian Institution Press, 1991). Other studies that discuss the development of visual claiming of the American landscape, although in different ways, include Angela Miller, Empire of the Eye: Landscape Representation and American Cultural Politics, 1825-1875, (Ithaca: Cornell University Press, 1993); and William Truettner, ed., The West As America: Reinterpreting Images of the Frontier (Washington and London: Smithsonian Institution Press, 1991).

9. See Joni L. Kinsey, Rebecca Roberts, and Robert Sayre, "Prairie Prospects: The Aesthetics of Plainness,"in Robert F. Sayre, ed. Recovering the Prairie, pp. 14-46. This article originally appeared in Prospects: A Journal of American Cultural Studies, 1996.

10. An extended discussion of this provocative assertion lies beyond the scope of this paper, but essentially I am claiming that all attempts to deal with prairie

landscapes, both historic and contemporary and ranging from the disparate developments of settlement, agriculture, industry, etc., are on some level based on aesthetic perceptions of the land and its potential or lack thereof.

11. For all their significance these artists remain underresearched. For more on them, however, see Kenneth Haltman, Figures in a Western Landscape: Reading the Art of Titian Ramsay Peale From the Long Expedition to the Rocky Mountains, 1819-1820 (Ph.D. diss., Yale University, 1992); John Francis McDermott, "Samuel Seymour: Pioneer Artist of the Plains and Rockies," Annual Report of the Smithsonian Institution, 1950 (Washington: Government Printing Office, 1951), pp. 495-509; and Jessie Poesch, Titian Ramsay Peale (1799-1885) and His Journals from the Wilkes Expedition (Philadelphia: American Philosophical Society, 1961).

12. George Catlin, North American Indians, (Edinburgh, 1926 ed.), pp. 245-46.

13. Ibid., p. 261. In his castigation of the plains as "sterile," Catlin was, of course echoing the common perception of the region as the "Great American Desert." This appelation originated with Stephen Long in 1821, but Zebulon Pike had been equally insistent on the matter in 1810. While it is easy today to dismiss such misconceptions as ignorant, as William Goetzmann has pointed out, at the time, without the technological developments that would later enable the prairies and plains to be settled, the early descriptions were apt. William Goetzmann, Exploration and Empire: The Explorer and the Scientist in the Winning of the American West (1967, repr. ed. Austin: University of Texas Press, 1993), p. 62. The desert/garden paradox of the plains has, of course, been discussed by many. For a substantial bibliography see John L. Allen, "The Garden-Desert Continuum: Competing Views of the Great Plains in the Nineteenth Century," Great Plains Quarterly 5 (Fall 1985): 207-220.

14. The definitive study of Miller is Ron Tyler, ed., Alfred Jacob Miller: Artist on the Oregon Trail (Fort Worth: Amon Carter Museum, 1982).

15. Miller's image was based on the actual experience of one of the Stewart party who became lost and nearly died. For more details see Tyler, Alfred Jacob Miller, text accompanying plate 52, not paginated.

16. Catlin, pp. 245-46.

17. A case in point are the exotic landscapes of Frederic Church in the late 1850s and 1860s which were unconventional in their compositions (especially Niagara, 1857, Corcoran Museum of Art) and in their subject matter (as in his tropical pictures and his arctic ones). These paintings, and others like them by artists such as Albert Bierstadt and Thomas Moran, capitalized on the taste for the unusual and were enormously popular.

18. Triptychs are three panels conjoined or exhibited as a unit. Traditionally this form was reserved for altarpieces or other similarly important forms of display. Although Hays's work is clearly not the former, it is significant that he found his subject imposing enough to require such extended treatment. The works are The Herd on the Move (1861, Thomas Gilcrease Institute of American History and Art, Tulsa, Oklahoma), The Stampede (or The Buffalo Hunt, 1862, Glenbow Museum, Calgary), and Herd of Bison Crossing the Missouri (1863, Buffalo Bill Historical Center, Cody, Wyoming). See Robert Taft, Artists and Illustrators of

the Old West, 1850-1900 (Princeton: Princeton University Press, 1953), pp. 41, 47-51. I am grateful to Gerald Carr for first bringing this to my attention and for his generous sharing of information.

19. Worthington Whittredge, The Autobiography of Worthington Whittredge, 1820-1910, ed. John Baur (1942, repr. ed. New York: Arno Press, 1969), p . 45.

20. Ibid., p. 46.

21. See for example Henry Nash Smith, "The Garden and the Desert," ch. 16 in Virgin Land: The American West as Symbol and Myth (Cambridge: Harvard University Press, 1950), repr. ed., 1970), pp. 175-83; and more recently John L. Allen, "The Garden-Desert Continuum: Competing Views of the Great Plains in the Nineteenth-Century," Great Plains Quarterly 5 (Fall 1985): 207-220.

22. While windmills had been produced in the East since at least the 1850s, it was not until the early 1870s that midwestern manufacturers began large scale distribution in the prairie plains region. Walter Prescott Webb, The Great Plains (1931, repr. ed, Lincoln and London: University of Nebraska Press, 1981), pp. 333-341; and more recently T. Lindsay Baker, "Irrigating With Windmills on the Great Plains," Great Plains Quarterly 9 (Fall 1989): 216-230.

23. Smith, Virgin Land, p. 175.

24. Henry Nash Smith, "Rain Follows the Plow: The Notion of Increased Rainfall for the Great Plains, 1844-1880," Huntington Library Quarterly 10 (February 1947): 169-93.

25. Bess Streeter Aldrich, A Lantern In Her Hand (New York and London: D. Appleton & Co., 1928). Little is known of Cover's life, but for more on her see William H. Truettner, The West As America: Reinterpreting Images of the Frontier (Washington and London: Smithsonian Institution Press, 1991), pp. 227-28, 351.

26. Discussions of women in the prairies and plains has been more extensive by historians and literary scholars than by art historians. See for example Julie Roy Jeffrey, Frontier Women: The Trans-Mississippi West, 1840-1880 (New York: Hill and Wang, 1979); idem, "There is Some Splendid Scenery: Women's Responses to the Great Plains Landscape." Great Plains Quarterly 8 (Spring 1988): 69-78; and Glenda Riley, The Female Frontier: A Comparative View of Women on the Prairie and Plains (Lawrence: University Press of Kansas, 1988). The contributions of women artists in the American West is treated in Patricia Trenton, ed., Independent Spirits: Women Painters of the American West (Berkeley: University of California Press, 1995).

27. For more on Wood see Wanda Corn, Grant Wood: The Regionalist Vision (New Haven: Yale University Press, 1983), and James M. Dennis, Grant Wood: A Study in American Art and Culture (Columbia. University of Missouri Press, 1987). For Hogue see Lea Rosson DeLong, Nature's Forms/Nature's Forces: The Art of Alexandre Hogue (Norman and Tulsa: The University of Oklahoma Press and Philbrook Art Center, 1984).

28. Annette Kolodny, The Lay of the Land. Metaphor as Experience and History in American Life and Letters (Chapel Hill: University of North Carolina Press, 1975); Smith, Virgin Land. The American West as Symbol and Myth.

29. Wood painted the picture for the Iowa State Fair and at its close Marshall Fields III purchased the work. Deere & Co. acquired the picture from the Field

collection in 1966. I am grateful to Lawrence Jonson, former curator of the Deere Art Collection for his correspondence with me about this painting.

30. Charles Dickens, "A Jaunt to the Looking-Glass Prairie and Back," American Notes: A Journey (1842, repr. ed. New York: Fromm International Publishing Co., 1985), pp. 177-184.

31. Theodore Winthrop from St. Louis to Frederic Church in New York, April 25, 1857. Olana State Historical Society, Hudson, NY. Frederic Church Papers, Letters Received.

GEORGE

Mary Swander

Uncle George smoked short
cigars and the night he died,
flicking ash on the floor,
said, "Reach under the cot,
honey, pull me out a beer."
Because he weighed only three pounds
at birth, Grandma kept him
in the oven for warmth,
and you still use the cake pan
she lay him in. At ten
he was kicked in the face
while castrating a horse
and George had one
glass eye from then on.
Winters, before a blizzard,
the socket throbbed and stung,
the lid rolling down like
a shade holding out the wind.
Summers, before a thunderstorm,
the eye swelled and blinked
up at you from the kitchen counter—
George afraid it would
explode in his head.

George smoked short cigars
and ground them out in
chicken-pecked barnyards while
the auctioneer waved his cane

through the air over:
milk cans and lard tins,
bridles and buckets,
buttons, thread,
First National Bank calendars,
hooks, rugs, ropes, pulleys,
hardback books on piglets and scours.

Five, five who'll give
me five, give me five?

George bid a dollar
on a windowpane and

One, one, I got one, one,
one, who'll make it two?

another on an incubator,
and two on a weather vane,
but he didn't need the brass rooster
spinning round to know that
in the distance clouds were
charging across the fields.

(We'd just left the sale,"
Edith Hill said in the World Herald,
"when we lifted into the air—
our old Chevy carried nearly
five miles—and would you believe it?
When we set down, we set down
right in front of our own house.")

And he didn't need the rooster
to tell him that Lyle Donavan
would keep up his song—
while the sky flashed yellow,
flashed purple—until every
last item was gone. So,
George waited, hands in pockets,
his one good eye on the horizon
while the other bidders
hugged the ground in the ditches
or ran for the cellar,
door slamming shut.
Later, through the rain,
you helped George pull home
a whole hayrack full
of loot for ten.

George smoked short cigars
and Grandma always cursed
and blamed them for sparking
the fire that burned down
all the buildings on the home place.
George squeezed his treasures
into a barn long since abandoned
by the cows, and their stalls
filled with washtubs,
hospital beds, a stuffed
two-headed calf.
Then every Sunday after dinner,
he disappeared to tinker:
nuts and bolts, a piece of wire,

copper kettle with coil.
"A little alcohol makes
a tractor run smoother."
George grinned at the heifer.
Soon, cars from all over
the county pulled into your lane,
headlights dim. Mason jars
glowed with the dark amber brew.
And because you were eight and
hands small, George had you
slips the extras into oil drums,
butter churns, and vacuum cleaner bags.
Once, when the sheriff came,
you even helped George into
the belly of an upright piano,
smoke rising from the lid.
"Put that out," you said,
and the strings twanged.
But you never saw smoke
rise so high, flames jumping
from barn to shed to house,
you never heard so many
buckets clank the night
the still blew.
Grandma leaned into the pump
and you ran water to the men
again and again, then
heard the rafters of the house
crack, tumble down through
the dining room,
felt the wind drive through

the grove, pushing the fire
into its own flame,
watched the moon rise over
the farm—George ambling down
the lane, to return only
one last time—and then all—
house, barn, shed,
piano, calf, coil—
collapsed into a circle of white ash.

JULIA
Mary Swander

Julia was the first
at ten—and the priest
rode all the way from
Omaha to bless the ground—
part of a pasture Grandpa
fenced in. When you were
born, her stone sank
deep into the grass,
but Grandma would still
sit up at night with
her pipe and tell the story.

Grandma:
Her body trembled so,
slow at first, then Lord,
I thought it'd never stop.
Mouth fell open, eyes
and tongue rolled back,
Poor wee thing,
You just never knew when.
Could be in the field,
the barn, kneeling down
for prayers. . . Just like
the horses Jim brought home.
Each week he hitched up
a new one to my wagon.
Most trotted along fine,
then I'd be headed off to town

and all I'd remember were
my hands gripping the reins,
knuckles white, the stallions
bolting through the weeds. . .
We had to pick her up
from the floor, slip a
strap around each thigh,
pull it tight—that sent
the blood to her head—
and soon she lay limp
in my arms. In Ireland
they said the tinkers
stole those babies and
set them up in front
of the church with a cup.
So, I always kept her close,
tucked under my arm,
braced against a hip—
even though there was
none of that here—
or so I thought. Once,
when she was just beginning
to teeter around
the sod shanty,
I heard scuffling and
shuffling outside.
The door flew open and
four tall Sioux walked in.
A man scooped her up,
pulled off her clothes
and handed her around—

first to the men,
then the women,
two of each—until
the last wrapped her
in a buffalo blanket and
plunkered her in my arms.
They left without saying
a thing, dropping a bag
of herbs on the bed: cinquefoil,
snakeroot and basswood leaves,
all to stop her shaking.
And they did.
She grew tall and thin,
then her heart began
to swell, to swell up
bigger than one of those
basswood leaves. You could
almost feel it open up
larger each spring,
push against her chest.
We were supposed to keep
her calm, but she was
always slipping off
to the barn trying to break
the ponies, tying their
tails together until
they kicked and bucked
until they finally gave up.
We tried to keep her calm,
hold her down, but it
was like the way

those Sioux made rope.
They stripped bark from
trees and soaked it
in a kettle with ash.
Time and again, it'd float
to the top until they
weighed it with a stone,
and even then they'd find it
bobbing back. They used bark
for bandages, too,
but a forest couldn't cover
the wound I felt the day
the ground opened and
the ropes lowered her coffin.
My first daughter gone.
And the old life, too.
They said those tinkers
dug up their dead and
carried them with them.
But I knew then we'd build
a frame house here, plant
a grove for a windbreak.
On these plains there were
so few precious trees.

The Commute of the Canadian Geese: The Search for Home

Thomas K. Dean

The choir of apple trees surrounds me with a sweet red chorus of September Song. I pause and watch as my wife Susan, my seven-year-old son Nathaniel, and my three-year-old daughter Sylvia quietly pull red globes from low branches. I listen to delicate stem snaps, the muffled drops of autumn fruit into dry baskets, and the slight swoosh of leaves as branches return to their natural resting spots. I gaze down into the valley of this orchard in eastern Iowa, through a scrim of misty humidity gently dropped upon the rolling vista. The undulations of the hills that nurture these apple trees resonated in Grant Wood's and Marvin Cone's eyes before mine. I revel in these gentle, primal shapes of the eastern Iowa river valleys, the smoky smells of September, and the crunchy bites of families enjoying the season's largesse.

A note sounds in the harvest orchard, at first dissonant counterpoint, an off-key, harsh punctuation. As I look skyward to spot its origin, the sound coalesces into a chorus. To the north, I see an awkward, wavering V-shape of disconnected black specks. As the bleating grows louder, the specks manifest form and motion. A flock of Canadian geese is flying over us. In Iowa, as well as throughout the Midwest, fall and spring bring these visitors. On crackling orange autumn mornings and sweetly cool spring evenings, the sky fills with this plaintive honking, pulsating rhythms audible from afar. The sound is the herald of the semi-annual commute of the Canadian geese.

My wife and children stop their apple-picking and join me in looking upward as the strident exhalations and intakes of resonant breath pass over us, the black necks with white rings snapping into visual relief. I feel as if I am enveloped in the formation's slowly-flapping wings. My daughter covers her ears as the honking fills the orchard, yet I open my soul to the benediction of the geese. It tells me that I have arrived home.

I experienced this tableau in the autumn of 1999, a month or two after a return to Iowa, to home. I was not born, nor raised, in Iowa. That part of my history belongs to neighboring Illinois. But if home is a place that grabs your heart and roots you in its soil with love, devotion, and longing, then Iowa is home to me. I lived in Iowa for five years from 1986 to 1991, and during that time, Susan and I cultivated an abiding affection for Iowa City, home of the University of Iowa where I was attending graduate school, as well as the gentle beauty of the landscape and the quiet dignity of the people of the state. We felt rooted, connected by spirit and desire, to this place in which we dwelled, for perhaps ineffable but nevertheless palpable reasons. As a "born and bred" Midwesterner, I had the rivers, valleys, fields, and woods of the middle land's landscape imprinted upon me from the beginning. Yet eastern Iowa seized my senses, my heart, and my soul, and wouldn't let go. The subtle grandeur of a river valley viewed from the top of a modest hill, the warm sunsets that painted trees and buildings in luminescent sharp relief (a special phenomenon of Iowa that Susan and I continue to call the "golden glow" of Iowa), the far vista of green corn fields gently rocking in the liquid July breeze: all these tableaux exalted my constitutional native Midwesternness into something that can only be called love.

For the last several years, the commute of the Canadian geese has been a sounding note of my subsequent search for home after leaving Iowa. In most ways, the idea of "commute" is anathema to me. Perhaps it was in my experience as a commuter that the seeds of passion for place were germinated. I have come to believe that rootedness in place is a fundamental necessity. The strongest human and cultural identity, the most insoluble bonds of community, and the most honorific relationship to the creation that is nature, can be best fostered through bedrock layers of unchanging constants, primary among them a persistent devotion to dwelling in a particular place. We need anchors in life—we need roots. Our lives change: our bodies change, our minds change, our politics change, our relationships change. Rootedness helps us weather the storms of change, holding at bay the empty despair of the anxiety of disconnection. Family and religion are constants for many people, rhizomes holding fast to people and spirit. Yet such powerful loves, and such strong roots, should also be extended into place, into ground, where roots most naturally and abundantly prosper, where they can drink of the most powerful, affecting, and abiding sources of orientation in our lives.

And that is why "commute" is anathema. Fundamentally, "commute" means change. While life needs change in many of its facets, relationship to place needs tending and nurturing over time. When change overwhelms place, the effect is deleterious, in the sense that it "deletes" place. In modern parlance, "commute" means to shift location between work and home; the greater the distance between the two, the more apt the term "commute." Contemporary America splits work and home, splitting our lives to no good end. A coherence in our lifeways is missing. Our work, our vocation, our "voice" in the world, should be one of the deepest expressions of our purpose on this earth, as are our human and spiritual relationships. A synergy between all these relationships—as can happen with the farmer, the teacher, the artist, the small business owner, for example—provides a powerful harmony to life that confirms its meaning. When that synergy is coherent with the place in which it is activated, no celestial alignment can compete with the power of such a harmonic convergence.

I have already confessed that I was once a commuter. For four years, I taught at a small liberal arts college in the northern suburbs of Milwaukee, Wisconsin. The saddest part of this situation for me was the placelessness of this school. The monochromaticism of American suburbia, with its endless off-the-rack houses, strip malls, and gas stations, is the major culprit of what James Howard Kunstler calls "the geography of nowhere." "Nowheresville," as far as I'm concerned, is no place to locate a school, or at least, selfishly, any school at which I would wish to work. I felt cast adrift in my days there. The Franciscan order of sisters who had founded the school resided on the opposite end of town. At five o'clock, the faculty scattered to the four corners of a million-plus metropolitan area, in their cars, of course. The students, mostly from working and middle class families, never had any hope of living in the wealthy suburbs where the school was located. I felt uneasy living with this disconnection between school and place, and more personally between work and home. I was used to communities where the town was, in many ways, defined by the institution of which I was a part. The scale of these towns, as well as the spirit, fostered inextricable links between work, community, and home life. Students, professors, and employees were neighbors as well as colleagues. In my interview at the suburban Milwaukee college, I asked the Dean of Students about the institution's place in the Milwaukee area. Her reply, shadowed by a slight laugh, was, "If we fell into Lake Michigan, no one in Milwaukee would even notice." Milwaukee is built on a marsh, and at the moment of that statement I felt this institution's tenuous relation to place, its lack of roots, most palpably.

I spent the next four years in a quest for place. After about a year of suburban living, imprisoned in a tomb-like apartment overlooking the expressway, waking every weekday morning to the clash of commuters clogging the eight lanes of concrete outside my window, Susan and I decided that we had to go further away to find a "real place," a real place to call home. We left suburbia for the small town, a little burg called Jackson, about twenty-five miles away.

In many ways, Jackson was much more a real place than Glendale/Fox Point (my school literally straddled two suburbs, enhancing its placelessness). Many of its residents had in fact lived in Jackson all their lives. I grew to know the names and faces of the clerks behind the post office counter. The pizza place we frequented was indigenous, not a franchise serving cardboard sameness, but a family-owned eatery, a little rough around the edges, willing to serve us a pie with a bubble of cheese that would have violated corporate standards in the bland world of chains.

But it quickly became clear to us that Jackson was no longer a small town. It was an ex-urb, the sprouting phenomenon of suburban creep. I should have known when, while changing the address on my checking account in the city, the clerk said, "Jackson—gosh, everyone seems to be moving there." An ex-urb: a place beyond the suburbs, the locus of new migration. A "city on the move," as the town elders proudly said, slapping that tired and meaningless, yet portentous, slogan on the sign at the city limits, short-sightedly rubbing their hands over the development and property tax dollars rolling in.

But the "movement" of suburbanization is suffocation. A Dairy Queen franchise goes up on the edge of town, just off the expressway that had been recently widened all the way to West Bend. No doubt McDonald's or Burger King now "conveniently" sits beside it. Condominium after condominium sprouted up near the wooded creek, beckoning clueless post-suburbanites who want to get "back to nature." The expanded video section of the enlarged Piggly Wiggly supermarket did serious damage to the small local video rental place down the street. After a couple of years, my rent went up dramatically. My landlord, living in the other half of the duplex, stood dumbfounded on the back porch as he served me notice, incredulous that his property taxes had doubled. He stared off into the cornfield that abutted our back yard, the cornfield with a "for sale" sign next to it at the highway, the cornfield that had already been platted as a grid of streets on the town map in the telephone directory, an invitation for more pre-fabricated architecture to be occupied by ex-urbanites. Well, that's progress. "A city on the move." It was happening. The place was becoming placeless.

Sadly, I must confess that I was part of the problem. I was really doing nothing different from what all the rest of the new residents were doing—escaping the dismal urban center and cloying suburbia. Those "other people" perhaps didn't have the sensitivity to preserving the uniqueness of the place (I thought, arrogantly), but I did enjoy an occasional Blizzard at the Dairy Queen, and I shopped at the Piggly Wiggly superstore, and I used the expressway at the edge of town to go to the mall, and even Wal-Mart occasionally.

Like a good ex-urbanite in a strange land, I even complained to the police one night when loud blasts peppered the darkness. "What the heck is going on?! It's disturbing my sleep!" It was the farmer down the road, who had started up his sound cannon that he had used for many a year to keep raccoons out of his field.

But most significantly, I did what most of the town did—I commuted. Every day, I burned gallons of non-renewable, polluting fossil fuel and made the twenty-five mile trip into the suburbs, spending at least eight hours a day in a place remote from my home, and a place remote from anywhere meaningful unto itself. I contributed to the clog of cars on the concrete strip that I despised so much when I had looked out my old apartment window every morning. Sometimes people in Jackson would ask me where I worked, and when I told them, they stared at me blankly, not even knowing such an institution existed. I felt the school was placeless to begin with, and here I was contributing further to its nowhere character, living my private life even more remotely from it, among people who hadn't the foggiest notion that the college even existed.

Two years later, we moved back to the suburbs, to a town called Brown Deer—and, of course, there was nary a brown deer to be sighted within its arbitrary borders. This was a move of defeat rather than a continuation of the quest for place. Despite the Welcome Wagon woman's visit to our house to give us coupons to the friendly businesses in our new "community" (most of them chain stores), despite our proximity to the local high school and library, a suburb is a suburb is a suburb. At least I didn't have to commute anymore.

Yet thinking back on that daily twenty-five-mile sojourn from the ex-urbs to the suburbs did help me, in some respects, feel a sense of belonging more effectively than my later cookie-cutter life in the cul-de-sacs of Brown Deer. Half of my commute from Jackson was on Highway 61, a state road that was still relatively rural. But the road was threatened by widening when we moved to Brown Deer, which would pave the way for the development steamroller between the two expressways that bounded my thirteen-mile commute across old 61. Every day, I at least saw—if only briefly, and if only at sixty miles an hour—some beautiful semi-rural Wisconsin landscape. I still remember the pumpkin patch at the corner of 61 and County T, following its rhythms for two years of growth and harvest, joyful one year as some young men created a deliciously autumnal pile of orange on the bed of their truck, saddened the next damp year at the number of stunted green balls left to rot in the bleak, yet still oddly beautiful, gray field of chill November mist. I remember fondly a quaint stone house, nestled in a field of strangely mixed prairie grasses and cattails, a sign at the road to the house announcing a loving appellation—the Pleiades. I daily envisioned clear, crisp nights in that field, staring at the carpet of stars above.

These images, however, were just that—fleeting images. I had no real connection to these landscapes, no roots to hold me there. I did not, in fact, spend any evenings in that field staring at those stars. I did not plant, nurture, nor pick any of those pumpkins. I hadn't the slightest clue what it meant to dwell in, to live in, to inhabit those patches of Wisconsin countryside. I zoomed past them twice a day, catching two-second glimpses, pasting those blurred, fractured images into a shallow scrapbook in my mind, a landscape of hurried imagination, an inchoate portrait of what I hoped life might be like. This is the curse of the commuter—a life of speed, blurred images. A life of disconnection, of incoherence between work, life, and place. There is no time to love place, to know it, to dig in, to get dirty, to grow deeply. There is only empty travel through and beyond. There is only nowhere. There is only rootlessness. And yet I did take something permanent away from this life of commuting, this path of broken lifeways. I took away a lesson, a lesson about what it means to dwell in place. The daily commute taught me that what I was doing was the precise opposite of creating a coherent life connected to place. My teachers were the Canadian geese. And, ironically, it was their commute that showed me the emptiness of mine.

As I said earlier, things do change, and sometimes life, and with it relationship to place, are defined by those changes. The Canada goose responds to climatic change. The Mississippi Valley population of Canada geese, which numbers around one million, migrate, or commute, yearly between Canada's Hudson Bay and southern Illinois. In spring, as the days begin to grow longer, they depart from their warm winter grounds to return to their Canadian breeding grounds. Eastern Wisconsin, a land of marshes and fields, is an ideal place for the geese to stop for a while—around two months—to partake of the abundant food in the wetland habitat that will fuel the remainder of their journey north. As April nights become longer and warmer, the geese depart for the land to the north, arriving in time for the available nesting sites delivered by melting snow in the Hudson Bay region. As the short sub-Arctic summer passes, the geese introduce their new families to the traces of the flyways that will chart their lives: the fall migration south begins. Once again, the geese make an extended one- to two-month stopover in Wisconsin and other upper Midwestern regions, enjoying the last remnants of the agricultural and wetland autumn bounty before making the rest of their way back to southern Illinois.

The Horicon Marsh, about fifty miles northwest of Jackson, is one of the major attractions for the Canada goose and other migratory birds. It is one of the largest coherent, protected marshlands in the country, consisting of 31,000 acres of open water and cattail marsh. It is a paradise of delectable food and shelter for the Mississippi Valley Population, and upwards of 200,000, or 20%, of the entire MVP call Horicon Marsh home at the peak of residency. Visitors from miles around come to the marsh in early morning and evening to be enveloped by astonishing sights and sounds of a fifth of a million geese arising, singing, and taking flight for a day of foraging in the morning, or the same number returning in the evening, alighting on the marsh in a massively growing choir of celebratory honking. During the day, the Horicon geese scatter about the southeastern Wisconsin region, and many others, perhaps not so inclined toward the natural equivalent of an urban center, choose to make their places in smaller nearby venues. Jackson, in fact, has its own small marsh and a number of small lakes in the vicinity, making the area inviting enough to create its own resident goose population. In the autumn and spring, then, my life in Jackson was accompanied by regular flyovers of singles, pairs, and V-formations of the large, black-hooded geese, the sounds of highway traffic and fall harvesters, or spring tractors tilling the fields, punctuated by a low bourdon of insistent bleating.

With a yearning for some sort of connection to the natural life about me while living in Jackson, I began paying close attention to the commute of the Canadian geese. These were creatures in complete harmony with their environment. Even though they were temporary residents, there was a permanence in the assuredness and regularity of their seasonal stopovers. In its flights across the blue, cloud-scudded Wisconsin skies, in its flapping landings in boggy marshes and open fields, the Canada goose was centered, and it experienced an intimacy with the land it knew well, a coherence with an ecosystem that provided beautifully for its instinctual needs. The Canada goose, in short, knew this place, lived in it, dwelled in it.

Fortunately, these ruminations about the geese helped provide me with a small sense of belonging, of connection to an environment that I tended to see as placeless and growing ever more so. I recall especially the evening of the first benediction, as I came to call it. By this time, my own family had grown, and Susan and I were walking along the highway with our baby son Nathaniel, returning from the Piggly Wiggly. It was early fall, and thankfully there were no trucks rumbling toward the expressway at the other end of town. All was unusually quiet. The sun was setting, mottling the purpling sky with amber and pink. The rare but characteristic perfection of autumn evening air that just gently cooled the nostrils gave our jacketless skin the slightest of shivers. We heard the tell-tale approach of rhythmic honking.

It was a rather large flock in V-formation, perhaps fifteen, even twenty geese, flying low. We all stopped and looked up. As they grew closer and flew above us, the plaintive honkings were accompanied by a low descant of flapping wings, a deep, rich whistling sound. I felt safe and comforted at that moment, almost as if the geese were wrapping us in their wings, even bestowing a benediction, a blessing of place, the assurance that placefulness existed because they were enacting it at that very moment. Although we could not follow the geese as they passed over us, I knew that they were going to a place in which they knew how to live—some nearby pond, or maybe even a marshy spot on a farm, maybe Horicon. And even though they would be heading further south soon, they would be back next spring, and fall, and spring again, to continue their ritual of rest and rejuvenation.

After this experience, flyovers have conjured that evening on the highway, and I have recalled, even during chaotic times, the tranquility of the geese plying the flyways of their lives. I especially remember one specific incident while commuting. There I was again, doing sixty-one on Highway 61, early in the morning, on the way to work. I was heading east, toward Lake Michigan, but I would turn off before I got there, onto the monstrous I-94 expressway that would take me south into the suburbs. In the distance, I saw a large formation flying toward me out of the north. Our paths would cross. As we intersected, as I zoomed under the formation, I even heard, fleetingly, the bleat of their honking. On the one hand, I felt kinship—we were all commuting together, beginning our days of work and providence. And yet, deep in my heart, and very quickly on the surface of my mind, I knew that we were flying at cross-purposes. That our paths crossed—they flying south, I flying east in my car—made it clear we were not doing the same thing. From the sky, the geese, their own wings propelling them in concert with the natural air surrounding them, had a coherent view of the broad landscape of mixed fields, marshes, and woods beneath them. I, on the other hand, traveling within a metal box at inhuman speed, merely saw incoherent flashes of pumpkin patches, stone houses in cattails and fields, whooshing past my window. The geese were going about their occupations in tandem with the natural environment—flying, even at speeds approaching my own automobile's, to the field or marsh that would fuel them for a long-range flight back home to their nesting ground. I was going to an occupation that I would abruptly cease at 5:00 p.m., disconnected from the land I dwelled upon, with no discernible connection to the longer rhythms of my private life of family and dwelling. The geese were flying in the well-carved grooves of instinct, keeping the way open for their future progeny. I was flying down a bed of concrete, arbitrarily placed on top of the natural undulations of the landscape, harming the environment in which my progeny were to grow up. Our paths crossed. Our purposes crossed. My commute was not their commute.

In succeeding years, before the return to Iowa, I still searched for place. After we moved to suburban Brown Deer, and as my son grew up a little, I continued to be reminded of the lesson of the commute of the Canadian geese, even though I myself was no longer a commuter. I was, however, a suburbanite once again. As we would hear the approaching honks over our house, sadly less frequent than when we lived in Jackson, Nathaniel would run outside to see the "gooses" fly overhead. They never flew as low or as benedictorily as they did that night in Jackson, but I was happy to see them fly over us at all, reminding me of the possibility of dwelling in place in this world. I was even happy to wash their prolific droppings off the roof of our house, thinking of them as gifts of the natural processes of living bestowed upon our dwelling, our home in the suburbs.

After finally deciding that we could not make a place for ourselves in Milwaukee, we spent two years in Michigan, in East Lansing. There I recaptured, to some extent, a sense of place that I had been missing in urban/suburban/ex-urban Wisconsin. The rhythms and connections between home, school, work, town, and landscape, while not perfect, were much more comfortable and real, less alienated and disrupted. At Michigan State, I began teaching from the perspective of place, working with my students on the meanings of place and community in historical contexts and in concert with our real lives. One of the most rewarding moments of my teaching career happened there when a student approached me excitedly at the end of the semester. I had asked my first-year writing students to write all semester, from multiple perspectives and approaches, about one particular place that was meaningful to them. One young woman had chosen to write of a lake cabin owned by her aunt, who, unfortunately, was contemplating selling the family gathering place. My student was quite distraught at this prospect, yet at the end of the term, she came to me flush with excitement, for she had shared her semester's writing with her aunt, who, after seeing the deep love for this place bursting from her niece's essays, decided not to sell the cabin. My work had helped preserve a place in which some folks were deeply rooted. I could ask for no greater reward.

Over the two years in Michigan, my family grew familiar with the variegated local fields, rivers, lakes, woods, and marshes, almost a smorgasbord of all the Midwestern landscapes familiar to us. During this time, our family also grew, with the birth of our daughter Sylvia. Even more intently now, I yearned for well-worn grooves of coherent, persistent lifeways, in harmony with a known and loved environment so we would know who we were and where we were, which, to me, are much the same thing. I envy the Canadian geese who, after only two months or so of raising their young in Hudson Bay, take them so soon on their first journey through their regular life patterns and into the dwellings that will remain their homes for their entire lives. With a new baby daughter and a son then four, I was saddened that I had yet been unable to start them on a similar journey of consistency and coherence in place, establishing life links to their natural environments. The geese had taught me that, even though their lives are annually transient, even though they commute regularly, they do so within a larger scale of intimacy and regularity with the natural places that define and provide for their existence, both in their individual lives and across time as a species.

Too far east from the Mississippi flyways, I received the benediction only once during my two years in Michigan. In October, I stepped outside to walk to the bus, about 7:30 a.m. The air was cool, crisp, though somewhat damp, as it always tends to be in Michigan, hugged by great lakes. The rising sun was filtering beautiful pinks and yellows through the clouds into the emerging blue of the daytime sky. Traffic was light, so the neighborhood was quiet. And softly, in the distance, there it was. The quiet bleating, the rhythmic undulations of wings, the V-formation approaching in the sky, and, once again, the benediction of a beautiful, comforting flyover.

The two years following Michigan brought me and my family much further north and west, to Moorhead, Minnesota. It is in many ways a remote place, sharing the banks of the Red River of the North with Fargo, North Dakota. The Red River Valley brought me out of the world of marshes and lakes back into the flat landscapes of grasses and vistas, and my heart did thrill to the familiar smells of grass, grass, grass, and the panorama of sky, sky, sky. We certainly made efforts at rooting—joining a church, buying a house, a beautiful old Dutch Colonial in the heart of town, which had even once belonged to the mayor of Moorhead, an ophthalmologist with the endearing name of Bottolf T. Bottolfson. We visited the Prairie Home Cemetery and the graves of the Bottolfsons. We made friends. We prepared Nathaniel for kindergarten. We found a favorite cashier at Hornbacher's grocery store. I taught about this place, about the checkered history of Moorhead, its tradition of saloons and Norwegian immigrants. I taught the wonderful contemporary writers of western Minnesota and North Dakota: the Blys, Bill Holm, Paul Gruchow, Louise Erdrich.

But in many ways this faraway place, while familiar in certain respects, was alien. We were surrounded by wheat and sugar beets rather than corn. There were no maple trees. Summer humidity was a novelty. Midwestern flatness was taken to an imposing extreme here. Visits to family 500 miles away with small children in tow required two or three days of travel.

The Canadian geese still were part of the northern plains landscape, of course. We were still on the path of the commute. But being much closer to Hudson Bay than we ever had been, and being on the beginning and lee ends of the journey each fall and spring, Moorhead was not one of their major ports of call. I do recall one brief incident that approached the benediction that I sought. It was April, which indeed can be a cruel month in northwestern Minnesota. While most Midwesterners are anticipating the fabled April showers, we often had to contend yet with blizzards. Yet on this one day in April, as I was completing my morning walk to my office building, I heard the honking and saw the formation overhead. It was a shallower experience, however, than the others I had been used to, as if the benediction were traced on thin paper, or made perfunctory by the geese's exhaustion or eagerness to arrive, finally, at Hudson Bay. Certainly the geese were more distant in the sky than I was used to.

After two years, our hearts tugged us home. Love is inexorable, and our love for Iowa was no different. Making some sacrifices, in career, in economics, and in further disruption for our children, our family trekked south to the place my wife and I had found greatest happiness, and the place where we wanted to carve out life experience for our children. We went home, to Iowa.

After we had lived here only a few months, the calendar shifted its digits. The "2" at the beginning of the year looked strange, and the realization that we were entering a new century made the reminder of change palpable. I am not so naïve as to think that we had reentered some kind of Emerald City by returning to Iowa. Our children are growing swiftly, we have experienced a health crisis or two, and the Iowa and Iowa City we knew ten years ago are not quite the same.

But once again, the Canadian geese have taught me this lesson. It is late March in the year 2000, my wife's birthday. We are taking our children on a little nature walk, along a path by the Iowa River that Susan and I used to frequent when we lived here years ago. It's actually not a very pleasant walk. It is cold, the air spitting hard, sharp, staccato bits of rain at us. It is rather too windy, and Nathaniel complains that his ears hurt. The enclosed path we knew has been altered. The railroad company has cut away much of the growth and brush that ran parallel to the tracks next to this path. A number of trees along the riverbank have been downed, victims of a vicious windstorm that struck Iowa City two years ago, which sent ancient stalwart trees on the University campus tumbling and which shoved train cars off their tracks to dangle precariously off a bridge over the Iowa River. The path we are on is at the juncture of Iowa City and Coralville, the latter a "suburb" of Iowa City that has experienced explosive growth since our departure in 1991, including the Coral Ridge Mall, Iowa's largest, at the edge of Coralville, a palace for the corporate, the chain, the franchise, the epitome of the geography of nowhere. Across the river from us on this path is the peninsula, a previously undeveloped piece of land. On our walks on this path ten years ago, Susan and I would often see deer browsing in the distant field, plying the brush at the edge of the wood. This previous year, close to four hundred of those deer fell victim on that very spot across the river to a sharp-shooter hired out of New England, who was charged with the task of controlling the "pest" population of urban deer, even though it is the urban encroaching upon the deer's habitat and not vice versa. We now see bulldozers and a dirt swath cut through the trees across the river, the first soundings of "The Peninsula Project." There may be some redemption, however, in the fact that the city is planning here a "neo-traditional" neighborhood, with mixed housing and some commerce and services located amongst the residences, a nod to the principles of the New Urbansim. Nevertheless, "progress" is changing the landscape, "developing" rather than preserving it.

We are back home, and we are happy, despite the discomfort of what we feel, what we see, and what we know on this day in late March on the cusp of the new millennium. We received a gorgeous benediction last fall at the orchard, so we know all is well, really. And to remind us of that, we hear an approaching bleat, then another. It is spring, after all, and our priests of the flyways are returning.

We are blessed with a somewhat different lesson this time, however. There is no V, no flyover. We look out upon the river, and we take in the sight of a Canadian goose sliding from the air onto the slightly choppy surface of the Iowa River. It is followed by another, skimming into a perfect landing on the water, joining its companion. The pair is together, on the river that remains in place as a constant, though it is surrounded by many changes on its banks. The companion geese are together, as are we, in a place they know well, and in a place they return to each year, a place in which we will dwell, with love and with roots.

Even though the spring benediction varies from the normal pattern, and even disconcerts us, cloaked as it is in foul weather, the geese always have taught me that there is consistency in change. This late spring encounter has taught us the acceptance of change in the context of rootedness, but the following fall reaffirms consistency. For me, it reaffirms home.

On this early October day, we are walking a path in Iowa City's Mormon Handcart Park. Although Mormonism is galaxies away from my personal beliefs and experiences, I am deeply touched by what happened here in 1856. In that year, Iowa City was the terminus of the Chicago and Rock Island Railroad, the last outpost of modern transport for Westward migrants. Brigham Young had been in Utah since 1847, overseeing the massive migration of Mormons to their new-found holy ground. This spot on what is now called Clear Creek became the staging ground for thousands of Mormons on pilgrimage to Salt Lake, their new-found spiritual and physical home. Literally at the end of the line of the railroad, these intrepid devotees took up hand carts to walk the remaining 1200 miles of their quest, hauling their families and life belongings across the tallgrass prairies to the foot of the Rocky Mountains over the course of four months.

These devout people were in search of home, a place where they could live their lives of spirit in peace. Their road to home was full of tragedy and violence. Just 100 miles southwest of here, on the banks of the Mississippi, lies Nauvoo, Illinois, the site of an earlier Mormon colony, established after persecution drove the latter-day saints out of Missouri. After developing the 10th-largest city in the nation there, Joseph Smith, the first of Mormon saints, was assassinated in his new-found community in 1844. The city was completely evacuated of Mormons in 1846, and the gorgeous temple atop a bluff over the greatest of American rivers was burned to the ground by enraged locals who feared the encroachment of a new social, political, and spiritual power in what they saw as "their" town.

Ten years later, in 1856, undaunted, hundreds of Mormons continued to flow into the Midwest, to this spot where I stand today nearly 150 years later, only this time to embark on a perilous journey to their new home in Utah, a dwelling place borne of uncompromising spirit of devotion and tenacity of will. If anyone has something to teach about going home, it's the Mormons.

Over the course of the next two years, over 1000 pioneers staged their Westward trek from this very spot. I find it difficult to imagine the hardships they were to face. Today is a perfect early autumn day. The sun warms our souls at an ideal 75 degrees. The crisp golden hues of the enveloping fall trees almost sparkle as the breeze jostles branches into motion. The dry smells and sounds of fallen leaves sweetly burn our nostrils a bit. Sylvia and Nathaniel gallop along the path ahead of us, finding small benches in cozy cul-de-sacs to sit on. The ghosts of joyful homeseekers a century and a half past sing a descant to this bucolic fall scene. Adding to the preciousness of these sensations is the fact that the landscape that surrounds us on this trail—the oaks, hickories, maples, and basswoods on the slopes of this tiny riverbed, as well as the bloodroot, phlox, and bluebells that are dying away toward winter—remains mostly intact from the days of the mid-19th century. That is rare in Iowa, where only one-tenth of one percent of the native prairie landscape remains with us today at the doorstep of the 21st century.

Despite the tranquility of this natural beauty, and the song lines of home that are scored through this landscape, historical markers remind us of sacrifice and tragedy as we retrace the steps of encamped Mormons here in this place. For two months in each year of 1856 and 1857, the bustling mini-city was filled with excitement as the pilgrims prepared their carts. But at least half a dozen of those seekers died at camp, resting now forever right here under our feet. Near-starvation threatened many of the pioneers before they reached Salt Lake. An early winter storm in what is now Wyoming killed dozens.

Although the Mormons did not seek out this place in Iowa as home, nor root themselves here, this spot resonates with the strongest possible desire for purposeful place. In the most fundamental and deepest ways, it speaks to me of my arrival at *my* home here. I don't know if the Mormons, encamped here, heard the plaintive honking of migrating geese as they were about to take their first hard steps toward home. I don't know if they looked in the sky and saw the wavering V-formation so many decades ago.

But I do today. As my family and I revel in an exquisite fall day and commune with the spirit of place, I almost do not believe what tickles the fringes of my hearing. As always, it is quiet at first, though still sonorous and slightly dissonant. The specks appear in the northern sky, heading south, our way, soon to be past our way. The raspy honks grow louder, and, by now almost instinctually, the kids shout, "Geese!," and look up. We all do, as the Hudson Bay winged pilgrims pass over us, singing their lusty excitement at the prospect of gathering in community to teach their new young to forage in warm climes. The spirits of the Mormons in search of home and the chorus of the commuting Canadian geese coalesce into perfect temperament, the overtones of the blessing of place vibrating in my veins, singing in my soul. The spiritual pilgrims I honor today have found home far west of here. The geese I revel in today continue tracing their flyways of home to the north and south of here. I am grateful that I find myself rooted to this middle spot today, in Iowa, where these crossings ground me where I belong, at home.

Echo of the Plains

Steve Semken

"Colorado wouldn't be too bad if they'd just flatten it out and cut down all the trees"—Kansas saying

You think you know it all from time to time, think you've got all of the world under your fingernails, all organizedily neat and clean. I know I've thought this and you probably have to. Here on the Plains though I finally learned one more thing and that's you won't know all there is to know out here. For one thing, the wind alone contains more than the brain can ever figure out. And the wind's not even all that difficult a part of the whole place really, it's just a tiny detail. I mean, my friend D. Zyne from the wind swept plains says, "only blows twice a year, six months from the north and six months from the south." You'd think someone could figure out the possibilities here, but sure as high water it can't be done.

It's all been no more than breathing each breath individually. Connections have always taken care of themselves. Now that I can't walk well and tire easily others feel they need to wait on me, want to hear me speak. I don't want any excuses made for myself or my talking, but I have lived straight smack dab in the middle of what's real and what's not my whole life. The problem with this being that it's hard to place anything in perspective. When I go to telling a tall-tale story it leans too much on truth, when I try to explain the truth I end up fetching a tub of lies. The main thing is that I am not too smart about any of this; it's not something I try to do. There is also the idea that neither the truth nor make believe are really any better than one another in the first place (that's my way of living anyway). Usually it's wise to choose one or the other, at least so I've been told, but I never had a choice 'cause I've been living in Echoes, which is a plain way, or what you might call a region of space in and around me where I've been stuck between everything.

Not to get too deep here, but I will say that I've heard some people mention that God exists in the space between things. Now if this is so then I've been living inside God. But since I haven't ever experienced any real miracles I know of, just everyday wonders out here on this rolling, unrelenting land I figure that mostly I've been moving with angels and probably just watched over by the Gods. If that turns out to be the truth, I could live with that.

Another thing is this. If you really want to live someplace, find a home and not a hiding place you have to create that place and this means figuring out how to mix and match reality and hope, dreams and guts, honesty and love, secrets with news, and rain with seeds. Tree shade and prairie roots are good too.

If there's a story I never knew it. I just talk about the days I've had in Echoes. Most folks think this place is nothing but a stretch of flat stuff, yet in a day's walk I can spot the mounds and rolls of what I call good-sized mountains. Most of what I have around me is loads of empty space. I often try to think how things go about making sense out here. Friend Jenks says I think more than makes "good sense" to him.

Here in Echoes the weather is sort of a secret. Fact, we'd be famous for our weather if anyone knew about this place. What makes the secret that much better is we don't even try to hide it. Anyone who wants to know is welcome to come and get it.

I mean, the way the wind can get to swirling makes a mind's eyes screw up and blur. There's blood in addition to the weather, but that's something that gets to boiling inside me during a rain storm, or a burrowing stiff, hard tossed hail storm that rips the plants clean down to roots. I wouldn't say there gets to being a fever inside me. At times I feel like a closet of hot air such as inside a tornado, there's thunder and lightning knocking around in my senses with a vein of high blood pressure trying to climb a ladder to the sky.

How'd I get so wild blooded? Just by watching the world around me. Like one time, when I was at a spot I call the Mountain View, I watched the wind flatten the mountains all the way to the ground, really, bent them straight over nearly seven thousand feet. I came running back to Echoes kicking and honking like a mule, "Ye'aw shewouldaww sawn it Friend Jenks, Yehaw shouldaww sawn it!" I kept on saying.

Friend Jenks said something like, "Oinkey Doinkey Boinky Boy," shrugged his shoulders and walked away in disgust, "fool boy, fool boy," he was thinking about me I'm sure.

Then again, maybe there are stories everywhere. I've experienced something at almost every spot across the space of Echoes. Really, the most accurate character to use as a narrator would be my feet, since if it weren't for walking there would be no stories at all. Of course, since I don't speak good foot I use my brain, trying to translate as best I can, remembering all along that walking is the beginning and the end of everything here, one foot in front of the other, in front of the other, to the other, on into thoughts, hopes and activity. Just like echoes in their own right, like the space around me, like dreams and reality stewed and then boiled for good measure to make a savory story broth.

Another time when I went walking out to spy on the weather, to scrutinize the clouds and their airy-water forms, I found some answers on patterning. Not definite patterns mind you, but clues. I discovered that I could see the weather being made ahead of time. From the ridge I was standing on, which I now call Cloud Catcher, I could see a good swath of the place I know as Echoes. From this spot I found out that I could watch the wind, water, sun and air stir up the next days weather.

When I saw big splashing buckets of water being hauled up and emptied into the clouds, I was just about as sure as a sunrise that it was going to rain in a couple of days. This isn't something I'm trying to be proud of, I mean, just because I have a secret to believe doesn't mean I know anything another person can't. It's possible that I could have just been seeing, or imagining things. I'm the first to know that just thinking something doesn't come close to equaling reality, or even toward getting things done. All it really means is I have something I'm willing to feel certain about. You know what though? It did rain a couple days later. Hard, like buckets of water were being dropped from the sky.

Most of life, like I said, has to do with walking and the thing most often walked to and stood by, here in Echoes, are the deep, yellow colored trees of ironwood. These trees and their wood stand as columns of natural strength, like the talons of a falcon. In some ways the wood is our prairie "fools gold," although I'll tell you one thing now, I feel anything but a fool about ironwood. We use the stuff for crossbows, firewood, walking sticks, fences, frames, floors, siding, shingles, walls, dyes, ... heck, we even use it for gun barrels and food. Working with ironwood tends to bring about a lot of chopping, sawing and then, as a result, a fair amount of sharpening saw and ax blades.

Friend Jenks calls chopping ironwood, Busting Metal. We chop wood early nearly every morning and my favorite noises while working on the ironwood is the deep thunk of popping a thick piece of wood apart. As for the value of the work, the results are well worth the effort. There's the color yellow inside the ironwood which always interests me. Shake roofs made of the golden wood are just as beautiful as the grin of the Mona Lisa, and just about as sly. Using the wood for heat is unbelievably intense and secure during the winter.

As for a monopoly on the use for ironwood, me and Friend Jenks can't claim that. We know for certain that others know about how the wood, but then again, we don't hear much about anyone else actually using it. Well, except, I saw an ironwood bowl once, oh yeah and a bolo, but that's it. I can't say I blame anyone for avoiding the stuff, it's tough to use, rough to handle and brutal to form. Personally though, I don't know what I would do without it. It's always been with me.

Even when I was little I liked it. I used to say over and over, when folks asked me what I wanted to be when I grew up, that I wanted to be a well stacked cord of ironwood.

Friend Jenks has said many a time, "What'ud the point be in avoiding it? The stuff gives me what I want, a thing both hard and good." I suppose we're both a bit psycho, but if we're out in a field and we pop a saw blade half, or crack an ax in half, we both laugh and laugh. We can't help it, we think its funny. Fact, Friend Jenks wears a necklace of chipped axe bits, kind of like the teeth of a tiger or something.

One time me and Friend Jenks were walking out to hunt morel mushrooms and chop ironwood when Friend Jenks got to humming.

"Whatcha humming Friend Jenks," I asked.

"Clouds."

Hmmm.....," I said as we kept on walking. Then Friend Jenks changed the tune a bit, "Now what?" I asked.

"Ironwood growing in the dirt," he answered back.

"Oh."

"Full of vitamins it is," added Friend Jenks.

"I'd of guessed that," I said to him.

Now, it was on this trip out into Echoes that Friend Jenks chopped an explosion out of an ironwood tree. This explosion was a story to be told over and over again for years. It never made sense when it happened, in fact, even thinking it over the last thirty-eight years hasn't cleared anything up much. Telling it to folks makes them sneeze mostly, that is they fetch the sickness I call doubt in their minds and leave me wondering which works better, talking what people want to hear, or telling what I remember happening. I usually get interrupted anyway before I ever finish with some kind of question. "Now where was it you said you'd lived?"

"Echoes," I'll say.

"What was the noise bouncing off to make echoes?" people will reply.

"No no, I mean I was living in a part of the world which is known as Echoes. The part, I suppose, you could say I've always heard the best. Or, maybe it's just the loads of empty space that make me say these things?."

"Oh."

This last, "Oh," always meant the end of any conversation.

To tell about the explosion though ... like I said, Friend Jenks and me were on our way to chop wood, or Bust Metal, when Friend Jenks spotted an ironwood tree he wanted to down for a joist in a barn he was planning on putting together.

So we walked on over to the tree, up a small rise, down into a slightly hidden draw all full of wonders and touching the tree, Friend Jenks measured the girth to see how this tree might work out. "Big enough to do the kitchen ceiling too," added Friend Jenks, pacing out another idea he'd just had on the ground.

"For certain on that," I added.

So Friend Jenks took his ax up over his shoulder and whacked the trunk a hard one, and that's when it happened. The noise of a thousand ricochets, a corp of drummers, two million Canada Geese sparked to flight, the bark of angry dogs across the world ... everything smacking at once.

The bash filled all of Echoes like it had never been filled before. Right then before us it was like we weren't living in Echoes any more since we were giving part of ourselves away. Heck, even the Filter River that runs through our basin flapped off the ground like a shirt pinned to a clothesline.

What blew from the trunk at first was a thing best described as ground, black peppercorn dust. A dark and grainy cloud of dry mist flew straight to our lungs and was sneezed out of us over the course of two more days.

As Friend Jenks and I traded continual sneezes, we peered through the pepper dust as it rose and whirled and spread through the sky. Then a gale force wind picked up and like a hardened knife cut the dust and spewed spirals across the ground. The space before us looked to be a field of human sized tornadoes in a state of fury.

While we watched the tiny tornadoes it started to rain. I mean really rain. I mean the kind of precipitation some people call cats and dogs falling from the sky. The kind of rain that we would later be able to tell grandchildren was a stick-to-the-ribs rain. Extra ordinarily large and heavy drops of water came whistled to the ground. We were bombarded by gallon sized drops of water for five days. No joke. Floods over floods. We took off for my house on a trot with our bags of morel mushrooms and axes in our hands.

"I guess I woke something inside that tree," said Friend Jenks during the third day of rain.

"Scared something out of the earth, would be more like it," I said.

"Of course, a rain like this makes you think we had it coming. Maybe some kind of cleaning is needed in our little world?" added Friend Jenks.

After it had rained five days the air slowed down and there was just a light mist falling. Everything outside seemed dead, drowned and dreary, completely quiet, all we heard was the dripping and sucking of water into mud. The earth had rolled over like ice on a winter lake. After what seemed like miles and eons of dripping water splating, soaking splashing the land Friend Jenks and I heard groans coming out of the earth. Noises that sounded of muffled rattlesnake tails shaking, or fresh beans bumping the sides of a can.

"I wouldn't say I know that sound right off the bat," quipped Friend Jenks.

"Sounds like the ground's got gas," I added.

"Think we might oughta wanna take a look around

now. Cure the curious brain you know," Friend Jenks said.

When the two of us ventured out the door and off the porch to look around we saw the giant earth worms.

We could hear them groaning, they looked like fish tossed on to land, left to flap and quiver, floundering helpless out of the dirt. We walked off the porch steps and stepped into the muddy ground, wherever we stepped there were squeals and moans like elephant snorts. They must have migrated up from deep in the earth. Friend Jenks stated his theory on these things, which was, they probably lived below the aquifer normally, but now they had to surface because of all the water. It's not everyday a theory like this comes in to use, but once Friend Jenks said it we stuck with it.

The worms were nearly seven feet long and a good foot an' a half in diameter. They had giant heads, with a host of squirming muscles that made them appear as strong as alloy router bits. They looked ancient. They were an eerie translucent color, soggy and rubbery, fully adapted to life underground.

"How long you think they been living?" asked Friend Jenks.

"Do I look like I'd know? These creatures probably been around ever since some God snapped their fingers and created the world I reckon," I replied.

"Kind of prairie specific no doubt, a smattering of the impossible if you get my drift," Friend Jenks professed.

We stared at the worms a long time and I started realizing that, in some ways, I would have been surprised if there hadn't been any worms swimming to the surface of the earth. That is to say, I have never seen trees cough pepper, rain fall for days like bombs, or soil turn over like pond ice. Thus, seeing giant worms rise from the earth, like glorious hump back whales, suddenly made a whole lot of sense to me. The size of the worms was the overwhelming part. I was certain that even a ninety pound catfish, lurking in the deepest channel of the mighty Mississippi River would have been too scared to try and eat, even approach, one of these giant crawlers. I guess that's how oddities exist. If something gets too big, too weird, even too fantastic it simply gets left alone, or on the other hand, misunderstood, just like Echoes and the plains.

After we'd been walking around a few hours, Friend Jenks pointed up and stated, "My o my, it's not raining anymore my good buddy."

It wasn't long after the mist stopped completely that the worms started digging back toward the core of the earth. As the last few worms were trying to squeeze back into the ground the sun came out and the sunlight seemed to magnify the worms strangeness. With cloud cover the worms made much more sense, their gray, thin skin merely seemed like an extension of mist, fog and rain. The sun seemed to shine right through them, revealing too much.

"Sound like a runaway freight train, eh?" declared Friend Jenks.

"More like an old man sneezing to me, just look at 'em drill back in the dirt," I said.

"Shoot, I'd be afraid of the sun too if I lived a mile

down in the ground," Friend Jenks professed.

Friend Jenks was probably right. We watched as sunlight covered the last of the giant worms. The heat from the sun made this last worm expand like a helium balloon though. Pretty soon it was ten feet off the ground. Then it burst and zoomed around as the air inside it was released. The worm casing landed near Friend Jenks feet. Curious, Friend Jenks picked it up, examined it for a moment then slipped the skin on top of my head like a stocking cap. He stood back, bowed and spoke, "Thou Are Now Kinged Holiest of thee Wormiest."

I felt mostly dumbfounded, but also a little prestigious too. Friend Jenks walked to his home afterward and I stood a little longer and thought about nothing in particular. I just tried listening to the earth. To the wind, the clouds, the water, and the leftover moonlight. I thought about the prairie roots, about the blue sky during daytime turning blackishpurple at night. My breathing was deep and I was glad the rain had stopped and that, with a few days of sun, I might be able to get back to my usual life.

I was, of course, still flabbergasted with the vision of the giant worms. I didn't really believe they existed in some way. But, then I remembered the worm skin over my head. I was glad to be wearing it and decided to leave it on.

As I watched Friend Jenks slipping back home through the mud I reached up to feel the worm skin on my head and thought about this place I've lived my whole life. I realized that even when I die something of me will remain. That the things I've done, like memories I have, will continue since what I do, what I see, what I think is how people live out here in open space. As well, I now believe that just as the Arctic has as much sunlight each year as the equator, so does Echoes have as much joy, happiness, love, sorrow and life as anywhere else, it's just spread out differently.

Photographer's Statement

Howard Vrankin

Many of us seem to value our connections with the wild. The prints for "Call of the Wild" were originally made while hiking, biking, and camping in southeastern Iowa, southwestern Minnesota, and western South Dakota.

During repeated and often extended solitary visits to the places photographed over seven years from 1994-2001 I came to deeply respect them as unique expressions of the Creator. I am beginning to understand how earth, sky, clouds, water, and all interrelated living things are, in many Native traditions, revered.

A photo is inherently interpretive. It never equals the original experience of reality. Rather a photo evolves through the necessary choice of film/digital medium, viewpoint, focus, exposure, enhancement, paper, dyes, and framing. In a sense, it becomes only itself.

If as interpretations of reality these photos help us to engage in meaningful conversations about the "Call of the Wild" then I will be doubly rewarded.

Palisades Kepler State Park
Mt. Vernon, Iowa

Restored Prairie at the
Herbert Hoover National Historic Site
West Branch, Iowa

Blue Mounds State Park
Luverne, Minnesota

Blue Mounds State Park
Luverne, Minnesota

Pipestone National Monument
Pipestone, Minnesota

Meet the contributors:

Mary Swander's most widely read books are her poetry collection Driving the Body Back and her memoir Out of this World. She is a native Iowan with an M.F.A. from the University of Iowa Writers Workshop. Ms. Swander teaches creative writing at Iowa State University when she's not raising vegetables and geese in Kalona, IA.

Howard Vrankin was born in Milwaukee, Wisconsin. Since graduating from Wartburg Theological Seminary in Dubuque in 1978, he has served a number of Evangelical Lutheran Church in America congregations in Iowa. He is married to Marcia Vrankin and the couple has two grown children, Heidi in Iowa City, and Peter in Burt, Iowa. A self-taught serious amateur photographer, Howard includes a number of his latest digital nature photos in this year's Harvest Symposium exhibit.

Steve Semken has called Iowa home for 28 of his 37 years of life. He has written three books on sense-of-place (The Tin Prayer, Moving With The Elements and River Tips and Tree Trunks) as well as edited one biography on retired, eccentric Midwestern, regionalist artist and college instructor Jack Ozegovic from Michigan (Northern Spirits Distilled). In addition he operates the Ice Cube Press in North Liberty, Iowa and also founded the Harvest Lecture four years ago. Steve lives with his wife Laura Waldo-Semken a local artist (artwork included in this book) and their 17 month old daughter, a true champion of play, Fenna.

Joni L. Kinsey is an Associate Professor of Art History at the University of Iowa where she specializes in American art, especially nineteenth century landscapes and imagery of the West. She is the author of Thomas Moran and the

Surveying of the American West (Smithsonian Institution Press, 1992), Plain Pictures: Images of the American Prairie (Smithsonian Institution Press, 1996) and The Majesty of the Grand Canyon: 150 Years in Art (First Glance Books, 1998). A native Oklahoman with roots in the tallgrass region of Osage county, she has had a life-long interest in prairies.

Thomas Dean, a dweller in Iowa City, Iowa, is Special Assistant to the President for communications and research at the University of Iowa. A native of Illinois, he returned to Iowa in 1999, unable to shake his love for the state after graduate school at the UI from 1986-1991. From 1991-1999, he taught at Cardinal Stritch College in Milwaukee, Wisconsin; Michigan State University in East Lansing, Michigan; and Moorhead State University in Moorhead, Minnesota. Dean has written numerous articles and given presentations on American literature, the pedagogy of place, and Midwestern regionalism. He is married to Susan Prepejchal, an English as a Second Language teacher. They are parents of two rascally but wonderful children, Nathaniel (9) and Sylvia (5).

Robert Sayre has been a tireless advocate for historic preservation, recreational trails, and prairie restoration. Along with the numerous scholarly books and articles he published during his career, he also took the initiative in the 1980s to compile the first Iowa guidebook since the WPA Guide of the 1930s. He edited and wrote part of Take This Exit as well as authored Take The Next Exit.

Paul Gruchow Author, editor, and conservationist who lives in northern Minnesota. His book Journal of a Prairie Year had its beginnings in a course he taught on the literature of the prairie at Worthington Community College. He is also the author of a splendid collection of writing entitled Grass Roots: The Universe of Home (Milkweed, 1995) as well as The Necessity of Empty Places (St. Martin's Press, 1988). He is a frequent contributor to the *Utne Reader*, the *New York Times*, the *Hungry Mind Review* and other periodicals.

Printer's Device designed by Andy Driscoll

Established in 1993, the Ice Cube Press is a small independent press dedicated to publishing writing on nature, the environment and Midwestern regionalism. Please order any of the books below.

River Tips and Tree Trunks:
$14.95 ISBN 1-888160-63-2
Essays and meditations on the flow of water, the growth of trees and flight of the blue heron.

Moving With The Elements
$14.95 ISBN 1-888160-35-7
Stories, essays and weather reports on fire, water, earth and air, plus eccentric hearsay.

Northern Spirits Distilled by Jack Ozegovic
$16.95 ISBN 1-888160-53-5
A collection of personal memories of eccentric, heroic people in the Upper Midwest, A full and powerful tribute to regionalism!

The Tin Prayer: Words of the Wolverine
Steve Semken
$11.95 ISBN 1-888160-01-2
A *regionalist manifesto* written while writer-in-resident at the Island Institute in Sitka, Alaska.

To order Ice Cube Press books send checks, or money orders to & include $1.50 handling:
Ice Cube Press
205 North Front Street
North Liberty, Iowa 52317-9302
icecube@inav.net www.icecubepress.com